D1483265

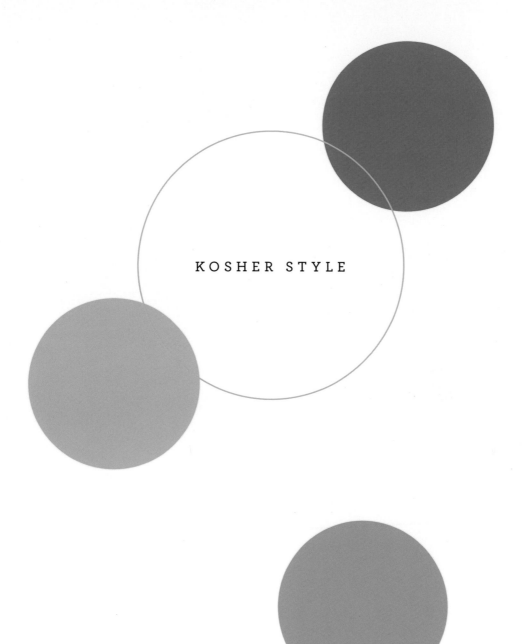

KOSHER STYLE

Kosher Style

More than 100 Jewish Recipes
for the Modern Cook

AMY ROSEN

appetite
by RANDOM HOUSE

Appetite by Random House™ and colophon are registered trademarks of Penguin Random House LLC.

Library and Archives Canada Cataloguing in Publication is available upon request.

ISBN: 978-0-525-60988-9
eBook ISBN: 978-0-525-60990-2

Cover and book design by Terri Nimmo
Photography by Ryan Szulc
Illustrations by Alanna Cavanagh
Printed and bound in China

Published in Canada by Appetite by Random House™, a division of Penguin Random House LLC.

www.penguinrandomhouse.ca

10 9 8 7 6 5 4 3 2 1

This book is for all
the *balabustas* of the world—
the Jewish women who have
made our houses into homes by
carrying on our culinary
traditions for generations.
Especially my mom.

Table of Contents

The author on the eve of her eldest brother's bar mitzvah.

Introduction

Our bubbes and boobies, saftas and nanas are the matriarchs of the kitchen and thus the rulers of the roost in Jewish homes. They are culinary giants in quilted polyester muumuus and silk slippers who know how to make the Semitic linchpins we grew up on—the kugel, the gefilte fish and the crispy-skinned roasted chicken. Sad to say, they won't be around forever, and that will be a loss indeed. But it will be an even bigger loss if the recipes we grew up on pass away with them, along with those special connections to our past.

Over a recent bowl of excellent matzo ball soup, I got to thinking: this generation is in real danger of losing the Friday-night dinner memories and a giant piece of our collective heritage. The dishes for celebrations and the ones for every day (though in Jewish homes, food is always a celebration). So I put down my soup spoon and picked up my pen. I was going to save Judaism! Well, maybe "save" is a little strong, but I decided the time had come for me to write the cookbook I've wanted to write for a decade. I have a sense of pride in my Judaism—what we eat is who we are. Obviously I'm not the only one who feels this way, as most people love the food of their people. But a lot of those people also happen to love the food of *my* people.

Sure, the food may not always look so hot—it was created to sustain, not to entertain—but it tastes like gold and oozes warmth. Through centuries of persecution, it's one of the things that has lasted, that has bound Jews together, our plates piled high with fresh blueberry blintzes. It still does.

From my Bubi Fran and Boobie Ronnie, to my mom and other cherished family and friends, everyone has their specialties. I've been eating and loving their dishes (and now missing some of them) my whole life, and with this cookbook, I'm taking these traditions and spiriting them into the 21st century.

Do me a favor and flip to the photo of the bagel, lox and cream cheese (p. 33). It's a thing of beauty—fresh cream cheese schmeared over a bagel with honey-mustard gravlax for a classic nosh. But here's the thing: in this book, not only will you learn how to make the bagels, you'll also learn how to make the cream cheese and gravlax. Keep on flipping and soon enough you'll see that my brisket is bathed and braised in maple and soy (p. 188) and that there's chocolate babka for dessert (p. 211). This reflects how I eat (I literally eat a bagel, lox and cream cheese every day) and how most of my Jewish friends and family eat. Traditional, but not outdated. These are living recipes.

"All of the dishes in this

book are inspired by

the tables and tales and

the chutzpah of the

North American Jewish

experience."

All of the dishes in this book are inspired by the tables and tales and chutzpah of the North American Jewish experience, and they represent what I think it means to be Jewish today. Using religion as a touchstone, all of the recipes also happen to be kosher (but more on that a little later).

Woven throughout are stories about my experiences as a travel writer with one of the most quotable populations on earth. From St. John's to Fort Lauderdale, Montreal to Manhattan, I've enjoyed meals and moments unique to the Ashkenazi experience, complete with humor, wisdom and chopped liver.

Kosher Style is for those who love delicious modern food, travel writing or both. It's a cookbook with food writing that respects the traditions born in eastern European kitchens, while traveling beyond. Jewish readers will love it for the taste memories they can recreate, while others will be won over by the gorgeous full-color photography.

So why is it called *Kosher Style*? Excellent question. While dozens of countries host at least a small Jewish population, the global community is concentrated in two areas. Israel and the United States account for 83 percent of the global Jewish population, with about seven million in each. Canada is home to about 500,000 Jews. A chunk of this global population of Jews is kosher, but even more of them are what we call "kosher style."

"Kosher style" is how many Jews eat today. This can mean dining on a smoked meat sandwich at a non-kosher deli, or eating a slice of sour cream coffee cake after you've had steak for dinner. It can mean Chinese food on paper plates in your home, or a lobster dinner eaten out while on vacation. For many, being Jewish tends to be more about culture than *kashrut* (the practice of keeping kosher), and it can be confusing at the best of times. I'll get into the rules of *kashrut* on page 4. But first, let it be known that this book isn't just for Jews. It's also for the other 99 percent of the population.

Recent market research studies peg the kosher-food industry as being worth over $17 billion, and the kosher label's popularity is growing. In 2009, 27 percent of packaged foods had the kosher denotation, but by 2015, it appeared on over 41 percent of packages. It's not that the world has suddenly gone *meshugenah* for kosher food. The reasons behind the dramatic uptick are completely nonreligious. Some people buy kosher food because of perceived cleanliness, others owing to dietary restrictions (such as vegetarians) and still others to avoid certain allergens such as shellfish.

In this book are all the recipes you need for successful shellfish- and pork-free home entertaining, be it for a Jewish holiday or a workaday dinner. From crave-worthy snacks to family-size salads, soulful mains to show-stopping desserts, all of the recipes in this book are doable in the home kitchen and are clearly marked as either a meat dish, dairy dish or pareve (neutral). Think: latkes, knishes, General Tso's chicken and Toblerone-chunk *hamantaschen* your family will *plotz* over.

Kosher Style is for anyone who likes to cook and loves to eat, and it's especially for those yearning to create new shared memories around a table brimming with history, loved ones and maple-soy brisket.

Ess, ess, mein kind! (Eat, eat, my child!)

Amy

Pareve   Dairy   Meat

On Eating Kosher

The rules of *kashrut* date back to biblical times, and the term refers to foods that follow Jewish dietary laws and practices. Literally, it means fit, proper or correct, and the actual biblical references, with specific details, are found in various verses of Leviticus 11 and Deuteronomy 14.

While the details of *kashrut* are extensive, the laws are all derived from a few fairly straightforward rules. Here are the biggies.

1. On three separate occasions, the Torah tells us not to "boil a kid in its mother's milk" (Exodus 23:19; Exodus 34:26; Deuteronomy 14:21). The Yiddish words *pareve* (neutral, like fruits or vegetables), *milchik* (dairy) and *fleishik* (meat) are commonly used to describe food or utensils that fall into one of those categories. Thus, you cannot serve milk with meat.

2. Certain animals may not be eaten at all. Some of you will say, "Well, okay, I didn't plan on eating a hyrax anyway because I don't know what that is," but remember that these rules date back to a time before factory farming. The animals deemed to be ritually impure include the camel, hyrax, hare and pig. (Beef, lamb, goat, deer and bison are all kosher.) All animals that can be eaten must chew their cud and have cloven hooves.

3. Of the animals that may be eaten, the birds and mammals must be killed in accordance with Jewish law, which includes draining all the blood from meat or poultry before it is eaten.

4. Certain parts of permitted animals may not be eaten.

5. All fruits and vegetables get the okay, but must be inspected for bugs, which cannot be eaten.

6. Meat (the flesh of mammals and birds) cannot be eaten with dairy. Fish, eggs, fruits, vegetables and grains can be eaten with either meat or dairy.

7. Of the creatures that live in the waters, anything that has fins and scales is kosher, but shellfish is forbidden. Fish like tuna, salmon, lake trout and herring are permitted.

8. Utensils (including pots and pans and other cooking surfaces) that have come into contact with meat may not be used with dairy, and vice versa. Utensils that come into contact with non-kosher food may not be used with kosher food.

Here's an example to help you get your head around *kashrut*. Let's say two cooks prepare two identical versions of chicken schnitzel: one of them kosher, the other kosher style. The kosher version starts with chicken that is slaughtered according to kosher dietary laws and purchased with very specific labels noting the kosher certification (COR; OU; or other accepted demarcations). Meanwhile, the kosher-style chicken can be purchased at any supermarket or butcher and lacks formal kosher designation.

The kosher recipe for these cutlets calls for moistening the chicken using either vegetable oil or a beaten egg. The kosher-style version could call for either of these ingredients, or it could call for the chicken to be dipped in milk. The kosher-style cutlets are then rolled in breadcrumbs or panko crumbs, which may be kosher or not. What makes the difference? The kosher crumbs are made of grains and may be seasoned. The non-kosher crumbs might include milk or some other dairy products, such as Parmigiano-Reggiano cheese. And if the crumbs are store-bought, they also may not have a kosher designation. It's all of the little things.

So what makes kosher style kosher? Absolutely nothing. "Kosher style" refers to foods that are traditionally served and eaten by Jewish people—primarily eastern Europeans, or Ashkenazim.

Any questions?

A Glossary of Jewish Terms

Many of Judaism's best-loved words are Yiddish, sprinkled about in conversations for emphasis or humor. The same goes for this cookbook. Some of the words have entered the common vernacular, but not all. So here's a cheat sheet.

Ashkenazi (plural Ashkenazim)

A member of one of the two great divisions of Jews. Ashkenazim are Jews of eastern European (Polish, Russian, etc.) lineage. The others, Sephardic (plural Sephardim), have roots in the Middle East and parts of Africa, including Morocco.

Balabusta

An especially gifted homemaker.

Bar or bat mitzvah

When Jewish boys and girls reach the age of 13, they read from the Torah (the bible) in synagogue and become full-fledged men and women with zits and braces, followed by a lovely party. A Jewish coming-of-age ritual.

Bisl (or bissel)

Bit—as in "a *bisl*" ("a bit").

Boychik

A boy, a young man.

Bubbe (or bubi, bubbie, bubby or boobie)

Jewish grandmother. We called mine Bubi Fran and Boobie Ronnie, so that's how I refer to my grandmothers in this cookbook. All others shall be referred to as bubbe.

Bubeleh

A term of endearment (although sometimes used in a patronizing way). "Honey, darling, sweetie, *bubeleh*."

Chutzpah

In English, chutzpah usually connotes courage or confidence, but among Yiddish speakers, it's no compliment. For the purposes of this book, though, it's a compliment.

Feh

An expression of disgust, representative of the sound of spitting, as in, "Did you see him in that tan leisure suit? Feh!"

Kashrut

The Jewish dietary laws and practices; see pages 4-5.

Kibitz

To joke around, have a laugh.

Klutz

A clumsy person, prone to breaking your prized glassware. Every family has one.

Kvetch

Both a verb and a noun, meaning to complain or whine. Or, as in, "He's such a kvetch." Every family has one.

Mazel tov

The congratulatory term to wish anyone well upon hearing good news—or when attending a wedding, a bris, a bar mitzvah and similar simchas.

Mensch

A good, honorable and decent person, as in, "He's such a mensch."

Meshugenah

Irrational, as in, "He's acting meshugenah!"

Mishpocheh

The family.

Nosh

A little nibble, a light snack.

Oy vey

An exclamation. The Jewish substitute for "Holy ——!"

Pisher (or pischer)

Often preceded by the word "little," as in, "He's such a little pisher." Someone young, inexperienced, not to be taken seriously.

Plotz

To go crazy because you love something so much.

Schmatas

Originally meaning rags, and still used as such when describing wiping down a table with a kitchen cloth. Also slang for garments produced at wholesale factories.

Schmuck

A foolish person.

Shalom

Peace, but also the Hebrew greeting for hello and goodbye (which is a form of peace).

Shiva

A weeklong mourning ritual in Judaism honoring the dead.

Shmaltzy

Related to the term "schmaltz," or chicken fat. In today's terms it means excessively sentimental or corny.

Shmoozer

Someone who's good at small talk, has the gift of the gab.

Shtetl

A small Jewish town or village, formerly found in eastern Europe, now (in a way) found in cities large and small around the world.

Shtick

Something you're known for; a gimmick done to draw attention. (*See* schmuck.)

Simcha

A Jewish celebration.

An Uncomplicated Pantry

The recipes in this cookbook don't call for many special ingredients, though there are a few. But before we go there, here are a few things I need you to know about the basics:

When I say flour, I mean all-purpose.
When I say eggs, I mean large.
When I say onions, I mean cooking (unless otherwise stated).
When I say milk, I mean 2% (unless otherwise stated).
When I say butter, I mean unsalted.
When I say sugar, I mean white granulated (unless otherwise stated).
When I say vanilla extract, I mean pure.
When I say pepper, I mean freshly cracked black.
The salt fluctuates between kosher and sea salt. (I let you know what's what.)
Herbs are fresh (unless otherwise stated).

Now, here are a handful of ingredients you may not be as familiar with:

Beet horseradish (aka *chrain*)
Jarred pickled minced horseradish, made crimson by the inclusion of beets. Usually served with gefilte fish.

Matzo
A dry-as-the-Negev unleavened bread that is traditionally eaten during Passover. Also used in cooking (see matzo *brei*, matzo balls, matzo pizza, matzo lasagna, matzo brownies and so on to eternity).

Pickled herring and onions
Where Sweden meets Poland in a jar of cured, pickled fish marinated in vinegar, herbs and onions. Find it near the refrigerated pickles in the supermarket.

Potato starch

This boxed product is a handy alternative to cornstarch during Passover, when corn is verboten.

Pressed cottage cheese

It's a soft, crumbly, very dry cottage cheese made from skim milk and pressed to remove almost all the liquid.

Russian-style mustard

Sweet and smooth, but also hot. Reminiscent of Chinese mustard mixed with honey.

Sour dills

Fermented in saltwater brine, these fat, juicy, garlicky dill pickles are the backbone of any deli meal.

Sweet kosher wine

Sweet sacramental wines, like those found under the Kedem and Manischewitz labels, are produced according to special dietary laws and are meant more for blessings than for pleasure.

Chapter 1

BRUNCH & SCHMEARS

(Pareve & Dairy)

The Early Bird Gets the Matzo Ball

"I don't know . . . the coffee makes me jittery."

"Put water in it."

"I don't know . . ."

"Try it. Just put water in it."

"Why doesn't she try the decaf?"

"I don't like it."

"Then try the water."

Overheard at Flakowitz, Boynton Beach, Florida.

They're popular and they're cheap. So why are Early Bird Specials frequented only by retirees of a certain age? Aren't they something we should all take advantage of now rather than waiting a few decades? This is my thinking as I enter Pomperdale, a New York–style deli in Fort Lauderdale.

I've officially begun my research into Early Birds—cut-rate dinners served between 3:30 p.m. and 5:45 p.m.—by eating a crack-of-dawn breakfast. Located in a strip mall, Pomperdale is a seemingly members-only deli with low ceilings and wood paneling. Its tightly packed tables are occupied almost exclusively by Jewish blue-hairs eating lightly toasted sesame seed bagels. These are my people, and this is our de facto Promised Land. I am confident they will help me in my Early Bird quest.

I take my seat and wait a few moments for menus to be delivered. "Oy, so cute!" shouts one old lady to the rest. "She thought someone was going to serve her!" Five minutes in and the Pomperdale clan has already labeled me adorable. "It's a crazy kind of place here," explains another. "You order up front, pour your own coffee, wrap up your leftovers and pay when you leave."

I *do* make several attempts to pour my own coffee, but a number of the Pomperdalians insist on doing this for me—even before I've wooed them with my prowess at canasta. Everyone here knows everyone: it's like *Cheers* for the geriatric set, albeit with no booze and a lot more Yiddish. Most Early Birds, they tell me, include a starter, a main course, a cold beverage (they ding you extra for coffee) and dessert. It's a huge amount of food for about $12.95. "And you can take home whatever you don't finish," someone proudly announces.

As I dig into scrambled eggs with Nova lox and onions that are a *bisl* cold and salty and are served on a paper plate with a plastic fork—not that I'm complaining, mind you— one woman suddenly pokes me and shouts, "They have the best chicken soup here! Oh my god, out of this world!" But there's a trick, she explains, now employing a whisper that is somehow louder than her speaking voice. "You order the matzo ball separately. That

way, there's no displacement of the soup!" I love this woman. When I ask her opinion on the best Early Birds in South Florida, the entire Pomperdale clan launches into a sort of vaudevillian act:

"J. Alexander's, Houston's, Sage . . ."

"Do you like Italian? Bon Gusto is *delicious.*"

"But they're closed on Mondays."

"Charley's Crab near Oakland Park . . ."

"Do you like fish? 15th Street Fisheries is very nice—a little expensive, but excellent service."

Later in the day, I head to 15th Street Fisheries, a legendary Early Bird eatery offering sunset dinners on the waterfront between 5 p.m. and 5:45 p.m. Located at the Lauderdale Marina, it has a setting that's flawless, but the room has seen better days— say, back in the early '80s. Still, for those who frequent Early Birds, the deal is more important than the decor or the food. Just like golf, schmaltz and shopping, it's a way of life.

The Pomperdalians were right that, at $18.95, the 15th Street Fisheries' Early Bird is pricier than most. But it gets you, among other things, the Fisheries salad: iceberg lettuce tossed with sliced strawberries, slivered almonds, crumbled bacon and baby shrimp, all coated in a sweet creamy dressing that proves that the grossest-sounding combinations are often the tastiest. Other high notes include an inspired intermezzo of ginger-orange sorbet and "bread girl" Meagan's sunflower-wheat and jalapeño-cheddar bread offerings. After

12.95

dinner, at 5:57 p.m., a woman with a towering blond bouffant and a yellow sweater with sequined panda bears brushes her teeth in the bathroom. She swooshes and spits, then turns to me. "They really give you a nice piece of fish here."

Another day, I visit Flakowitz, a deli and bakery in Boynton Beach with 70-year-old "bread boys." It's a home away from home for Jewish snowbirds who make sure they're seated by 4:30 p.m. for the Early Bird, which entitles them to precisely $1 off the main course.

We order chicken soup (matzo ball on the side, please), cabbage rolls and blintzes. Dinner arrives exactly two minutes later, and the bill a minute after that. Don't get me wrong. This abrupt service isn't insulting; that's just the way it's done here. Why wait when you could be eating? Why linger when you could be playing shuffleboard?

The soup—the color of a young hen—is wonderful, and the matzo ball properly yielding. The cheese blintzes have a crispy exterior with a warm, vanilla-scented filling. The cabbage rolls are sweet and sour, just like my Boobie Ronnie used to make. All told, it's the real deal.

I have to admit that the food tastes pretty great. Still, despite the deals, I think for now I'm willing to pay the extra buck to finish off the workday before heading to dinner. But a few decades from now, God willing, I can imagine myself here, *kibitzing* with pals— like the woman a few tables away, resting her foot on a chair while nibbling on rugelach. Although she appears to be in agony, by all accounts she's prone to histrionics.

"Oooh, oooooh," Mary groans.

"What's the matter with you?" Sol asks, with fake concern.

"Oohhh, I started limping yesterday."

"Well, you're limping better today."

I should only be so lucky.

Pickled Salmon

Some older family friends asked if I'd be including a recipe for pickled salmon, but I had never had it before. So I researched it, made it, tried it and decided that I love it. Lightly pickling the salmon makes for a subtly spiced, moist piece of fish. Spread some cream cheese on a bagel and eat a few chunks of pickled salmon and carrot on the side.

1 medium onion, sliced

1 lb fresh salmon, bones removed

2 large carrots, thickly sliced

¼ cup sugar

½ cup white vinegar

½ Tbsp sea salt

1 tsp pickling spice

½ cup water

1. Place the onion slices in a nonreactive pot, then place the salmon and carrots on top.

2. Add the sugar, vinegar, salt, pickling spice and the water to the pot. Bring to a boil, then lower heat and simmer, covered, for 25 minutes.

3. Cool the salmon in the marinade slightly on the counter, then refrigerate for 1 hour. Remove the salmon from the marinade, discard the skin and break the salmon into large chunks before serving.

Mom's Sweet Challah

"It's like cake!" is the standard exclamation whenever someone tries my mom's challah for the first time. Now it's a bit of a family joke to be the first one to shout it out at Rosh Hashanah, the Jewish New Year. Over the decades, my mom has become rightly famous for her large, round, sugar-topped loaves. She, along with her friend Marlene, makes challahs for about 20 households of family and friends who now expect this annual gift. Mom and Marlene wouldn't have it any other way.

FOR THE DOUGH:

1 (¼ oz) package quick-rise instant yeast

½ cup sugar, divided

2¾ cups warm water, divided

9 cups flour

1 Tbsp kosher salt

1 egg, beaten

⅓ cup vegetable oil, plus a drizzle for bowl

FOR THE TOPPING:

1 egg yolk mixed with 1 Tbsp water

½ cup brown sugar

1. For the dough, in a stand mixer with a dough hook, combine the yeast with 1 teaspoon sugar and ¼ cup warm water. Let stand until frothy, about 10 minutes.

2. Slowly add the 9 cups flour, the remaining sugar and the salt to the bowl, then add the egg, oil and remaining 2½ cups warm water. Mix at low speed for 3–5 minutes, until it comes together. Increase the speed to medium and knead for 7–8 minutes, until the dough is elastic and no longer sticky.

3. Place the dough in a large well-oiled bowl, turning the dough over to make sure it's fully coated in oil, and cover with a tea towel. Let stand for 1 hour, until doubled in size.

4. Line two rimmed baking sheets with parchment paper. Set aside.

5. Dust the counter with flour and punch the dough down. Divide into two equal portions, then roll each piece into a very thick rope and coil it around itself a couple of times, starting with the top tucked in and then tucking the bottom of the rope under each loaf, sort of like a squat beehive. Place each loaf on a prepared baking sheet. Cover with tea towels and let rise for another 1½ hours, until doubled in size.

(continued)

6. Preheat the oven to 350°F. Brush the egg yolk and water mixture all over the loaves. Sprinkle generously with brown sugar and pat the surface to make sure it sticks.

7. Bake the loaves one at a time, until golden brown and cooked through, about 35–40 minutes. When done, the loaves should sound hollow when tapped on the bottom. Transfer to a wire rack to cool completely.

Bialys: Soft Onion Buns

I read Mimi Sheraton's *The Bialy Eaters* a decade ago with an intensity not usually reserved for the history of an onion bun. But it wasn't until about a year ago when I finally tried one, at Russ & Daughters in New York, that I understood the appeal (aside from its interesting backstory). Soft and fresh, fluffy and oniony, they're like a cross between a bagel and an onion bun, and if you ask me, they're due a comeback. I'd file these under "weekend project," as they're easy to make but need several hours of rising time.

2 cups warm water, divided

1 (¼ oz) package active dry yeast

2 tsp sugar

2 tsp sea salt

5¼ cups flour

Drizzle of vegetable oil

FOR THE ONION TOPPING:

1 tsp olive oil

2 tsp poppy seeds

½ cup finely chopped red onion (about ½ small onion)

1 Tbsp dehydrated onion flakes

½ tsp kosher salt

1 egg, beaten, for egg wash

1. In the large bowl of a stand mixer, combine ½ cup water, the yeast and the sugar; let stand for 10 minutes, until foamy. Add the remaining 1½ cups water and the salt and flour. Knead with the dough hook on low speed for 8 minutes, until smooth. The dough should come away from the bowl but will be slightly sticky.

2. Form the dough into a ball and place in a large well-oiled bowl, turning the dough a few times to coat it in the oil. Cover with a tea towel and let rise for 1½ hours, until tripled in size. Then punch the dough down, flip it over in the bowl and cover with the towel again and let rise for another 45 minutes, until doubled in size.

3. To make the onion topping, combine the olive oil, poppy seeds, onions, dehydrated onion flakes and salt in a small bowl. Set aside.

(continued)

4. On a floured surface, punch the dough down and roll into a log. Cut the log into eight equal rounds. Lay the rounds flat on a lightly floured surface, cover with a tea towel and let rest for 10 minutes.

5. Line two baking sheets with parchment paper.

6. Pat each piece of rested dough into 3- or 4-inch rounds. Place the rounds on the prepared baking sheets, cover with tea towels and let rise for 30 minutes.

7. Preheat the oven to 425°F.

8. Make a large indentation in the center of each *bialy*, pressing down firmly from the center outward and leaving a 1-inch rim. Brush the *bialys* with egg wash. Place about 1 teaspoon onion topping in each indentation, pressing it down slightly with a spoon. Cover with tea towels and let rise for 15 minutes.

9. Bake on the upper and lower racks of the oven for 6 minutes, then switch the pans, rotate 180 degrees and bake for 7 minutes more, until lightly browned. Do not overbake. Cool on wire racks. If not eating immediately, place in plastic bags—a key step for the telltale soft crust. Otherwise, schmear away!

Joanna's Famous Granola

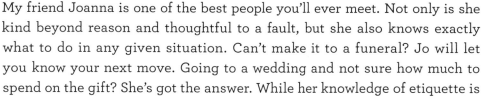

My friend Joanna is one of the best people you'll ever meet. Not only is she kind beyond reason and thoughtful to a fault, but she also knows exactly what to do in any given situation. Can't make it to a funeral? Jo will let you know your next move. Going to a wedding and not sure how much to spend on the gift? She's got the answer. While her knowledge of etiquette is peerless, Joanna is also an incredible cook, whipping up healthy, wholesome, tasty recipes for her family each and every day. To be honest, I'd hate her if I didn't love her. Joanna also has a great granola recipe (which she says she adapted from Early Birds Foods granola) that she's sharing with me for this cookbook. My one concern with this recipe is that Joanna may think that because I now have the secret, she can stop making the granola for me. This is not the case.

3 cups old-fashioned rolled oats

1½ cups pecans, coarsely chopped

1 cup hulled pumpkin seeds

1 cup hulled sunflower seeds

1 cup unsweetened coconut flakes

½ cup pure maple syrup

½ cup grapeseed oil

½ cup packed brown sugar

1½ tsp kosher salt

1. Preheat the oven to 300°F and line a rimmed baking sheet with parchment paper.

2. Place the oats, pecans, pumpkin seeds, sunflower seeds, coconut, syrup, oil, sugar and salt in a large bowl and mix until well combined. Spread the granola mixture in an even layer on the prepared baking sheet. Place in the oven and bake, stirring every 10 minutes, until the granola is toasted, about 45–55 minutes. The finished product should be golden brown.

3. Remove the granola from the oven and season with additional salt, if desired. Let cool completely before serving. Can be stored in an airtight container for up to 1 month.

Homemade Bagels

Easier than you'd think! More delicious than any you'll know! These bagels are a cross between a slightly sweet and chewy Montreal style and a petite, light Toronto Gryfe's bagel. In other words, they're the best of both worlds.

3½ cups flour

2 (¼ oz) packages active dry yeast

1½ tsp sea salt

1¼ cups warm water

½ cup honey, divided

Drizzle of vegetable oil

1 egg yolk beaten with 1 Tbsp water, for egg wash

¼ cup sesame or poppy seeds

1. In a stand mixer fitted with the dough hook, combine the flour, yeast and salt. Slowly add the water and ¼ cup honey. Knead on a low setting for 5 minutes, until the dough comes away from the sides and a soft, smooth ball forms.

2. Lightly oil a medium bowl, and place the dough ball inside, turning it over to make sure it's fully coated in oil. Cover with a damp tea towel and set aside in a warm place for 30 minutes.

3. Lightly flour a work surface and roll the dough into a long snake, then cut into 12 equal pieces. Roll each piece into a rope about 8–9 inches long. Pinch the ends together, then roll with the palm of your hand to seal the ends and form a bracelet— a bagel bracelet. Cover the bagels with a tea towel and let them rest on the floured surface for 15 minutes.

4. Place an oven rack on the lowest position and preheat the oven to 450°F. Line two baking sheets with parchment paper.

5. Bring a large pot of water (at least 10 cups) to a boil, and add the remaining ¼ cup honey. Lower the heat to a simmer, then add four bagels at a time, simmering for 2 minutes, flipping each one over, and simmering for 2 minutes more. Remove the bagels and place on the prepared baking sheets. Repeat with two more batches of four bagels at a time.

6. Divide the bagels equally between the prepared baking sheets. Brush with egg wash and sprinkle each bagel with some sesame or poppy seeds (or place the seeds on a plate and gently press the bagels, one at a time, into the seeds).

7. Bake one sheet at a time for 18–20 minutes, or until cooked through and deeply golden brown. Let cool, then slice and schmear! They also freeze well.

Homemade Cream Cheese

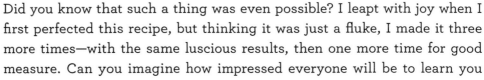

Did you know that such a thing was even possible? I leapt with joy when I first perfected this recipe, but thinking it was just a fluke, I made it three more times—with the same luscious results, then one more time for good measure. Can you imagine how impressed everyone will be to learn you made homemade cream cheese? "Get out of town!" they'll all shout. Little will they know it takes only about 5 minutes to make before draining overnight.

1 cup whipping cream

1 cup milk

1¼ cups 2% plain yogurt

½ tsp kosher salt

3 Tbsp white vinegar

1. In a saucepan over medium heat, whisk together the cream, milk, yogurt and salt. Bring to a boil, stirring constantly and making sure it doesn't boil over, for about 2 minutes. Add the vinegar, bring up to a rolling boil for 30 seconds, then lower the heat and let simmer for 3 minutes more. Remove from the heat and let cool for 1 hour.

2. Line a fine-mesh strainer with a clean cotton tea towel and place over a medium bowl. Pour the mixture into the lined strainer and cover with plastic wrap. Place in the fridge and let drain overnight.

3. Discard the liquid from the bowl and spoon your gorgeous, tangy cream cheese into an airtight container, stirring until smooth. It will keep in the fridge for up to 2 weeks.

Four Types of Schmears

When my roommates and I were at McGill University, each night without fail, someone would pose the 10 p.m. question: "Do you feel like sweet or salty?" It was snack-time at 99 Sherbrooke Street. "Sweet" meant heading out for cookies, frozen yogurt or ice cream, whereas "salty" usually meant staying put for bagels and schmears. Here's a blueprint for mixing it up at your brunch (or late-night snack) table. Your bagels will thank you.

Mixed Herb Cream Cheese

½ block (4 oz) cream cheese, softened

2 Tbsp chopped chives

1 Tbsp chopped flat-leaf parsley

1 Tbsp chopped basil

1 tsp lemon zest

Pinch of sea salt and pepper

Blend all the remaining ingredients into the cream cheese until smooth. Refrigerate for 1 hour to let flavors meld before serving.

Veggie Cream Cheese

½ block (4 oz) cream cheese, softened

4 green olives, chopped

1 green onion, trimmed and chopped

2 Tbsp finely chopped red pepper

2 Tbsp grated carrot

¼ tsp red pepper flakes

Place the softened cream cheese in a small bowl. Blend all the remaining ingredients into the cream cheese until smooth. Refrigerate for 1 hour to let flavors meld before serving.

(continued)

Salmon Spread

½ block (4 oz) cream cheese, softened

3 Tbsp finely chopped lox (smoked salmon)

2 Tbsp butter, softened

1 Tbsp fresh lemon juice

1 tsp chopped capers

Pinch of pepper

Place the softened cream cheese in a small bowl. Blend all the remaining ingredients into the cream cheese until smooth. Refrigerate for 1 hour to let flavors meld before serving.

Everything Bagel Schmear

½ block (4 oz) cream cheese, softened

1 Tbsp sesame seeds, toasted

1 Tbsp dehydrated onion flakes

½ Tbsp poppy seeds

¼ tsp garlic powder

Place the softened cream cheese in a small bowl. Blend all the remaining ingredients into the cream cheese until smooth. Refrigerate for 1 hour to let flavors meld before serving.

Sour Cream–Pecan Coffee Cake Muffins

When you're not having everyone over for mah-jongg but you still feel like a nice piece of cake, these muffins—moist, crumbly and crunchy—are like the best streusel-topped coffee cake you've ever had.

FOR THE TOPPING:

1 cup finely chopped pecans, toasted

¼ cup packed brown sugar

2 Tbsp sugar

1 tsp ground cinnamon

FOR THE BATTER:

1 cup butter, softened

½ cup sugar

2 eggs

½ cup full-fat sour cream

1 tsp vanilla extract

1½ cups flour

1 tsp baking powder

½ tsp baking soda

½ tsp sea salt

1. Preheat the oven to 375°F and line a 12-cup standard muffin tin with paper liners.

2. To make the topping, combine the pecans, both sugars and the cinnamon in a small bowl. Set aside.

3. For the batter, using a stand mixer, beat the butter with sugar until fluffy, about 3-4 minutes. Scrape down the sides and add the eggs, sour cream and vanilla.

4. Whisk together the flour, baking powder, baking soda and salt. Gradually beat into the butter mixture, scraping down the sides occasionally and making sure that everything is combined and fluffy.

5. Spoon 1 tablespoon batter into the bottom of each paper liner, then sprinkle each with 1 teaspoon pecan topping. Add another spoonful of batter to each liner, then sprinkle with the remaining topping.

6. Bake on the middle rack of the preheated oven for 20-22 minutes, or until a cake tester inserted in the center of a muffin comes out clean. Store at room temperature in your best airtight container for up to 2 days.

Farmer's Salad

An old-style deli-style cheese salad—it's more cheese than salad, and more delicious than not. It's a light yet fortifying lunch, a creamy mixture speckled with the crunch of radish and cucumber and the zest of lemon. It's an unusual combination that's as refreshing as a day at the beach, and a classic that belongs in this book. In other words, try it; you'll like it!

1 (18 oz) package pressed cottage cheese

1 cup sour cream

About 5 red radishes, trimmed and thinly sliced

½ English cucumber, peeled and diced

3 green onions, trimmed and thinly sliced

1 tsp lemon zest

Sea salt and pepper to taste

1. In a medium bowl, break up the pressed cottage cheese with a spoon, then stir in the sour cream to combine. Add the vegetables, lemon zest and seasonings. Mix well, then refrigerate for at least 1 hour before serving. This is great as a side to bagels or scooped on top of greens for a nice salad.

Cheese Blintzes with Blueberry Sauce

SERVES

6–8

A great dish for breaking the fast at Yom Kippur, or for Shavuot—a holiday commemorating the giving of the Torah to the Jewish people on Mount Sinai. Traditionally, dairy-only dishes are served for both holidays. With the tender crepes folded around a vanilla-scented cheese filling and topped with a fresh blueberry sauce, it's as decadent as a dessert but eats like a main.

FOR THE CREPES:

3 Tbsp butter, melted

4 eggs, beaten

1½ cups milk

2 cups flour

FOR THE FILLING:

3 cups pressed cottage cheese

2 egg yolks

3 Tbsp sugar

½ tsp vanilla extract

FOR THE BLUEBERRY SAUCE:

3 cups frozen blueberries, thawed and drained

½ cup sugar

1 Tbsp cornstarch

2 cups fresh blueberries

Vegetable oil, for frying the crepes

1 Tbsp butter, for frying the finished blintzes

Sour cream, for serving (optional)

1. For the crepes, in a medium bowl, whisk together the melted butter and eggs. Add the milk, then gradually add the flour, whisking until just blended. Let sit for 1 hour so the gluten can activate.

2. To make the filling, mix together the cottage cheese, egg yolks, sugar and vanilla until well combined. Set aside.

3. For the sauce, in a medium saucepan, combine the 3 cups previously frozen blueberries, sugar and cornstarch. Set over medium heat and stir until the sugar dissolves. Bring to a boil, stirring occasionally for 2–3 minutes, until the sauce thickens. Remove from the heat and add the fresh blueberries. Set aside.

4. Heat an 8-inch nonstick pan over medium heat. Using a pastry brush or paper towel, brush the pan with oil, then spoon about 3 tablespoons batter into the hot pan,

swirling the pan quickly to thinly coat the surface. Fry on one side until cooked and the top is dry, about 1–2 minutes. Turn the crepe out onto a clean tea towel, making sure the browned side is turned upward. Re-oil the pan for each crepe. You should have 16–18 crepes in the end.

5. Once all the crepes are cooked, fill each one with a heaping tablespoon of the cheese mixture along one edge, browned side up. Fold in the sides and roll up like a burrito. Repeat until all the crepes are filled.

6. When you're ready to serve, fry each blintz in butter until slightly crisp on both sides. Serve with the blueberry sauce and sour cream (if using).

Creamed Herring

Herring has its fans and its detractors, but I'll tell you this: at least a handful of people will be happy to see it on your brunch table, and I am one such person. Same goes for all Jewish men over the age of 70.

1 (13 oz) jar pickled herring and onions

1 cup full-fat sour cream

2 Tbsp finely chopped chives

1 Tbsp smooth Dijon mustard

Pepper

1. Drain the jar of herring and onions, reserving 4 tablespoons of pickling liquid. Place the liquid in a medium bowl, along with the sour cream, chives, mustard and a generous amount of pepper. Stir to combine, add the herring and onions to the bowl and toss to coat. Refrigerate overnight before serving.

Tuna Mousse

This is sort of a dip and sort of a mousse, kind of fancy but also not. Think: France meets a bagel brunch. It's familiar in taste if not in texture—lighter and more delicate than what you might expect. But I promise, you'll *amour* it.

½ cup whipping cream

1 (6 oz) can flaked white tuna in water, well drained

1 tsp lemon zest

1 Tbsp fresh lemon juice

2 Tbsp finely chopped chives

1 tsp smooth Dijon mustard

2 tsp chopped capers

Sea salt and pepper to taste

1. Using a wire whisk and a steady arm, whisk the cream until stiff peaks form.

2. In a separate bowl, combine the tuna, lemon zest and juice, chives, mustard, capers and salt and pepper. Mix well so that there aren't any large chunks of tuna.

3. Fold the tuna mixture into the whipped cream until combined. Cover and refrigerate for at least 1 hour so the flavors marry and the mixture firms up slightly. Serve with baguette or bagel slices, crackers or crisps.

Vegetarian "Chopped Liver"

I have many vegetarians in my life—if I'm being honest (and of course I am), perhaps too many vegetarians. This easy fake-out freaked them out, as they were convinced I was serving them real chopped liver, which I would never do. It's got all the flavor and texture of the real thing, including the disconcerting color! P.S. They loved it once they got over their initial fears.

3 eggs, room temperature

2 Tbsp olive oil

2 onions, chopped

Sea salt and pepper to taste

Pinch of sugar

1 cup walnut pieces, toasted

1 (19 oz) can green lentils, rinsed and drained

1. To hard-boil the eggs, bring a medium pot of water to a boil, add the eggs and lower heat to a simmer. Cook for 12 minutes. Remove from the heat, drain the water and fill the pot with cold water to stop the cooking. Peel the eggs and set aside.

2. Heat the oil in a skillet over medium-low. Sauté the chopped onions for 20–30 minutes, seasoning with salt and pepper and a pinch of sugar, until soft and caramelized.

3. In a food processor, pulse the nuts, then add the sautéed onions, hard-boiled eggs and lentils. Pulse, then process until the puree resembles chopped liver. Add more salt and pepper to taste and process again to blend. Refrigerate for at least 2 hours in an airtight container. Serve with crackers or matzo.

PB&J Bread Pudding

 Is it breakfast or dessert? You're both right!

2 eggs, beaten

½ cup sugar

¼ cup butter, melted and cooled

1 tsp vanilla extract

2 cups milk

1 small stale baguette, torn into small pieces (about 3–4 cups)

½ cup smooth peanut butter

½ cup raspberry jam

1. Preheat the oven to 350°F and butter an 8 × 8-inch ovenproof baking dish.

2. In a medium bowl, whisk together the eggs with the sugar, melted butter and vanilla until smooth. Whisk in the milk.

3. Place the prepared bread in the baking dish and pour the custard mixture overtop. Press the bread down with a spoon or spatula until it is nice and moist.

4. Using a soup spoon, drop dollops of peanut butter and jam equally overtop the bread pudding. Place on the middle rack in the preheated oven and bake for 50 minutes to 1 hour, until browned and bubbling. Let cool for 20 minutes before serving.

Honey-Mustard Gravlax

I've been making my own gravlax for years, and I encourage you to give it a try. It's a mostly hands-off endeavor, but there is a 48-hour plan-ahead time investment. With a steady hand for thin, careful slicing, this lox is the *cure* for your bagel and cream-cheese cravings.

2½–3 lb whole side skin-on salmon

1¼ lb kosher salt

2 lb sugar

½ cup liquid honey

2 Tbsp dry mustard

1 bunch dill, washed and well dried

1. Get out a baking sheet large enough to hold the salmon. Mix the salt and sugar together, then spread about half of the mixture on the bottom of the baking sheet. Place the salmon on top, skin side down, and evenly pour the honey on top of the fish. Sprinkle with dry mustard.

2. Completely cover the salmon with most of the remaining salt and sugar mixture (see note), carefully packing it down. No pink should be showing. Lay the dill over the salt and sugar (it will permeate), cover with plastic wrap and place at the back of the fridge for 48 hours.

3. After 2 days (it's worth it, I swear), the salmon is cured. Carefully wash off the salt and sugar with cool water and pat dry with paper towel.

4. To serve, thinly slice the salmon on the bias down to the skin, but don't slice into the skin. Serve as part of a lovely bagel brunch, with cream cheese, tomatoes, sliced cucumbers, thinly sliced red onions and capers.

Note: You may want to reserve a bit of the salt and sugar mixture to seal broken spots on the curing mixture, which can happen after about 12 hours.

Double-Decker Egg & Tuna Party Sandwiches

Somewhere along our culinary lineage, party sandwiches became the go-to nosh at daytime gatherings. I remember my Bubi Fran and her sisters rolling the sliced bread flat before filling the sandwiches and forming them into pinwheels or fingers. It took all day, but that was mostly because of all of the *kibitzing*.

2 loaves sturdy white or brown sandwich bread, sliced horizontally into ¼-inch slices (a bakery will do this for you)

FOR THE EGG SALAD:

6 eggs, room temperature

3 Tbsp mayonnaise

1 tsp smooth Dijon mustard

Sea salt and pepper to taste

FOR THE TUNA SALAD:

3 (6 oz) cans solid white tuna in water, drained

4 Tbsp mayonnaise

2 Tbsp sweet relish

Sea salt and pepper to taste

1. Carefully trim all of the crusts off the loaves of bread (save them for the birds). You should have pristine rectangles. Using a rolling pin, gently flatten each slice so that it's about half its original thickness. This will help make the sandwiches sturdy.

2. Bring a medium pot of water to a boil, then carefully add the eggs and lower heat to a simmer. Cook, uncovered, for 12 minutes. Remove from the stove and drain the hot water into the sink. Cover the eggs with cold water to stop the cooking. Let sit for about 10 minutes. Once cool, peel and grate the eggs into a medium bowl. Stir in the mayonnaise, Dijon and salt and pepper until smooth.

3. For the tuna salad, break up the tuna in a medium bowl using a fork, then stir in the mayonnaise, relish and salt and pepper until smooth.

4. Spread a few heaping tablespoons of egg salad on one slice of prepared bread, then smooth with a knife so it reaches the edges. Top with a second slice of bread, pressing down gently. Then top with a few heaping tablespoons of tuna salad, spreading to reach the edges. Top the tuna with a final layer of bread and press down gently. Wrap tightly in plastic wrap. Repeat the process with the remaining slices of bread and egg and tuna salads. Refrigerate for at least 2 hours before serving.

5. When ready to eat, unwrap and slice each large triple-decker sandwich into 1-inch-wide finger sandwiches. Let the party begin!

Charoset: Traditional Nut & Apple Spread

A key recipe for the Seder meal, *charoset* symbolizes the mortar that the Jews used to layer bricks when they were enslaved in ancient Egypt. It may not look like much, but it's delicious spread over matzo—a winning mix of apples, nuts and wine. When non-Jewish people are invited to a Seder, this is the taste they remember most.

2 green apples, peeled, cored and chopped

½ cup walnuts

¼ cup sweet kosher wine (such as Manischewitz or Kedem concord grape)

1 tsp ground cinnamon

2 tsp honey

1. Combine the apples, walnuts, wine, cinnamon and honey in a food processor and pulse until almost smooth—leave a bit of texture. Serve with matzo during Passover or anytime the craving strikes. Why limit yourself to Passover? This is good stuff!

Amy's Perfect Pecan Buns

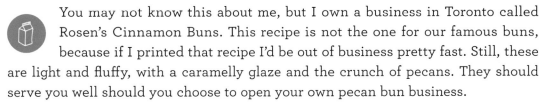

MAKES

12

You may not know this about me, but I own a business in Toronto called Rosen's Cinnamon Buns. This recipe is not the one for our famous buns, because if I printed that recipe I'd be out of business pretty fast. Still, these are light and fluffy, with a caramelly glaze and the crunch of pecans. They should serve you well should you choose to open your own pecan bun business.

FOR THE DOUGH:

1 cup milk

5 Tbsp butter

1 (¼ oz) package active dry yeast

3 Tbsp sugar

1 tsp sea salt

4¾ cups flour, divided

3 eggs

Drizzle of vegetable oil

FOR THE TOPPING:

¾ cup butter

¾ cup packed brown sugar

2 tsp ground cinnamon

½ cup chopped pecans

Pinch of kosher salt

FOR THE FILLING:

¾ cup brown sugar

½ cup chopped pecans

2 tsp ground cinnamon

¼ cup butter, softened

1. Make the dough. In a small saucepan over low heat (or carefully in the microwave), warm the milk and butter until the butter has melted and the temperature is hot but not scalding (you're looking for 105°F on a thermometer). Pour the mixture into the bowl of a stand mixer fitted with the dough hook, and sprinkle the yeast and sugar overtop. Do not stir. Let sit until it foams, about 8–10 minutes. Stir in the salt.

2. Add 2¼ cups flour and mix until just combined. Add the eggs and mix until incorporated. Knead the dough on medium-high speed until a smooth batter forms, about 2–3 minutes. Add the remaining 2½ cups flour and knead on medium until the dough comes together and forms a smooth, elastic ball, about 6–8 minutes. Add a bit more flour if needed.

(continued)

3. Add a drizzle of oil to a large bowl and turn the ball of dough around in it so it's got a light sheen all over. Cover the bowl with plastic wrap and let the dough rise until it doubles in size, about 1 hour.

4. While the dough is rising, make the topping. Grease a 9 × 13-inch baking pan with a bit of butter. Melt ¾ cup butter in a small saucepan over medium heat. Stir in the brown sugar and cinnamon, whisking until smooth. Pour into the greased baking pan. Sprinkle the bottom of the pan with chopped pecans and a pinch of salt. Set aside.

5. To make the filling, combine the brown sugar, chopped pecans and cinnamon in a bowl. Set aside.

6. When the dough is ready, punch it down and roll it out on a floured surface into a 12 × 18-inch rectangle. Spread the softened butter over the dough with an offset spatula, leaving a ¾-inch border along the sides. Sprinkle evenly with the brown sugar, cinnamon and pecan filling mixture.

7. Starting at one long end, roll the dough into a log and pinch to seal the seam. With the seam side down, slice the log into 12 fat rounds; each one should be just over three fingers thick. Place in the prepared pan, cut side up and slightly spaced apart. Loosely cover with plastic wrap and let rise until puffy, about 20–25 minutes.

8. During this second rise, place a rack in the center of the oven and preheat to 375°F.

9. Once the buns have risen, remove the plastic wrap and bake the buns until golden brown, about 18–22 minutes. Let cool in the pan for 3 minutes, then invert onto a serving platter. Scrape any remaining filling from the pan onto the buns. Serve at once. If you don't eat them all in one sitting, they also freeze well.

We invite you to Sabbath Services
Saturday, the twelfth of June
nineteen hundred and eighty-two
at nine o'clock in the morning
Beth Tikvah Synagogue
3080 Bayview Avenue
when our daughter
Amy Ruth
will be called to the Torah
as a Bat Mitzvah

We would be honoured
to have you share our Simcha
and join us for Luncheon after Services

Fred and Marsha Rosen

אביבה רחל רוזן
Amy Ruth Rosen

The author's bat mitzvah invitation.

Chapter 2

SOUPS & SUCH

(Pareve, Dairy & Meat)

Bagels Are the Best Cultural Unifier

I eat at least half a toasted bagel every single day. It is my lifeblood. It is my heritage. It is usually my breakfast.

There are many Jewish dairy restaurants in my hometown of Toronto that specialize in baked goods like bagels, challah, babka and the rest of it. Back at the turn of the 20th century, when boatloads of observant Jews were arriving from eastern Europe to escape persecution, "dairy" meant kosher (because no meat was in the mix, the fear of non-kosher meat, or the mixing of milk with meat, was eliminated), and kosher meant home. One restaurant that serves only dairy, United Bakers, was founded in 1912 and is still thriving, while Harbord Bakery has been baking the world's best challah and cheese Danishes since 1945. The city also has countless dedicated bagel spots, from Gryfe's to Bagel World to Bagel House to the new *pisher*, NU Bügel in Kensington Market, where Toronto's Jewry first laid roots.

In the mid-1990s, I was attending school in Halifax, Nova Scotia, for a journalism degree along with a tight class of about 36 students. Dave, a nice guy from a Toronto suburb, was one of them. I didn't eat pepperoni pizza and that's what the gang always ordered, so Dave, who I believe was secretly in love with me, always had a bagel and mini packet of spreadable cream cheese on hand for me in his dorm room. One evening, a bunch of us were gathered at Dave's for an impromptu post-exams pizza party, Dave dutifully preparing my bagel and schmear. All dark hair and deep brown eyes, he suddenly looked different to me.

Even in Halifax, where many pronounce them *bah-gel* (shudder), Dave knew that this was a meal I could eat and enjoy. He didn't steal those bagels from residence for himself; he stole them just for me. This was a guy who was thoughtful and giving and knew me so well. It might have been the cream cheese talking (though more likely the beer)—but it did make me wonder if he could he be my *beshert* (my destiny)?

Bagels unify us, their doughy circles connecting Jews like a chain-link fence across the Diaspora. There's breaking bread, and then there's breaking bagels. For non-Jews, it's the gateway drug to Jewish cuisine.

My friend Ilona is not Jewish but is deeply fascinated by Jewish food customs. I would go to a bar mitzvah brunch and she'd ask, "What did they serve?"

"Bagels, lox, cream cheese, tuna and egg," I'd say.

I'd go to a bris. "What did they serve?" she'd ask.

"Bagels, lox, cream cheese, tuna and egg," I'd say.

I'd go to a shiva. "What did they serve?" she'd ask.

After a while she just stopped asking.

But here's the thing: A fresh bagel is so delicious and comforting that it never gets stale. And once you try it with a fresh schmear and some lox, it's game over, *bubeleh*. You officially become part of the inner circle.

Cabbage Borscht

There was a lot riding on getting this dish right, as it was our favorite soup from my Bubi Fran. I started developing the recipe at the cottage last winter while most of the family was up north, as I needed their familiar taste buds. "Sweeter," said my brother Andrew. "More tomato," said my mom. After a pinch more of this and a *bisl* of that, my dad took a taste from the pot. "That's it." My heart swelled with pride.

1 Tbsp olive oil

1½ lb short ribs (*flanken*)

10 cups cold water

1 large onion

1 (28 oz) can whole peeled tomatoes in liquid

1 cup tomato sauce

1 tsp garlic powder

1 medium head cabbage, finely shredded (about 10 cups)

½ cup pitted prunes, finely chopped

Sea salt and pepper to taste

¾ cup packed brown sugar, or to taste

3 Tbsp red wine vinegar, or to taste

1. Heat the oil in a large stockpot over medium heat. Pat the meat dry with paper towel and sear in the oil for 2–3 minutes on each side, until browned. Add the cold water and bring to a boil, then lower heat and simmer for 30 minutes, skimming the top of the soup occasionally to remove any foam.

2. With a sharp knife, pierce the onion four or five times, then add it to the soup. Piercing it allows the flavor to permeate the soup without the onion falling apart.

3. Squeeze the canned tomatoes through your fingers and add them to the pot along with the liquid from the can. Add the tomato sauce, garlic powder, shredded cabbage, prunes and lots of salt and pepper to taste. Bring back to a boil, then lower heat to a simmer. Partially cover and cook for 1½ hours.

4. After 1½ hours, add the brown sugar and vinegar—you're looking for a nicely balanced sweet-and-sour taste. Simmer for 30 more minutes. Remove and discard the onion. Remove the short ribs, slice into large pieces, add back to the pot and serve.

Meat *Kreplach*

MAKES
ABOUT
4
DOZEN

It's no surprise that Jews love dumplings—have you ever been out for dim sum on a Sunday? But we also have a dumpling to call our own: *kreplach*, which is a nice change-up from the standard matzo ball. When you're taking the time to make dumplings, you don't just make a dozen. So settle in, put on some klezmer music and fold away. Your freezer (and future Shabbat dinners) will thank you.

FOR THE FILLING:

2 Tbsp olive oil

1 large onion, diced

1 lb lean ground veal

½ tsp sea salt

¼ tsp pepper

2 Tbsp finely chopped flat-leaf parsley

FOR THE DOUGH:

4 cups flour

1 tsp sea salt

2 eggs, beaten

2 Tbsp olive oil

1 cup boiling water

1. For the filling, heat the olive oil in a large skillet over medium-high heat. Sauté the onions until nicely browned, about 10 minutes. Remove with a slotted spoon and set aside. Add the meat and salt and pepper to the pan and sauté on high heat, stirring frequently, until all the meat is browned and crumbly, about 7–10 minutes. Add the onions back to the pan and stir for 1 minute to combine. Stir in the parsley and remove from the heat. Set aside.

2. To make the dough, using a stand mixture fitted with the dough hook, stir together the flour and salt. Add the eggs and oil. Then, on low speed, start drizzling in the boiling water, kneading until a stiff dough forms, about 5 minutes.

3. Lightly flour a work surface and divide the dough into four equal balls. Cover with a damp tea towel and let rest for 30 minutes.

4. To make the *kreplach*, add a touch more flour to the work surface. Roll out one of the dough balls into a rectangle about ⅛ inch thick (but really as thin as you can get it). Cut into 2-inch squares, then place 1 heaping teaspoon of the meat mixture in the

center of each square. Fold in half diagonally to make a triangle, pinching the edges firmly together. Bring the longest edges together and pinch to complete the *kreplach* (think: tortellini). Repeat with the remaining dough and filling.

5. To cook the *kreplach*, bring a very large pot of salted water to a boil (if you don't have a very large pot, it's best to do this in batches). Lower the heat to a gentle simmer, add the *kreplach* and cook, covered, for 20 minutes. Remove and drain. Serve the *kreplach* in chicken soup, or pan-fry with caramelized onions as a side dish. Cooled extras can be frozen flat in freezer bags and stored for future *kreplach* needs.

Green Onion Vichyssoise

Vichyssoise, a creamy, cold leek and potato soup, was a summertime tradition when I was growing up. My mom was into Julia Child, and this was the treat she'd bring up as part of our picnic lunch during visitors' day at Camp Shalom. I'm bringing back the good times with a green onion twist, because a classic is always timely.

6 or 7 green onions (usually 1 bunch), trimmed and cut in half

½ cup chopped flat-leaf parsley

1 Tbsp butter

1 small onion, sliced

2 medium Yukon Gold potatoes, peeled and thinly sliced

2 cups no-added-salt chicken or vegetable stock

1 cup whipping cream

Sea salt and pepper to taste

1. Bring a medium saucepan of salted water to a boil. Add the green onions and parsley and blanch for 30 seconds. Drain and immediately rinse in a strainer under cold water, then pat dry. Roughly chop and set aside.

2. In the same rinsed and dried saucepan, melt the butter over medium heat. Add the onions and cook until very soft but not browned, about 5 minutes, stirring often. Add the potatoes and stock. Bring to a boil, cover and lower the heat to a simmer for 25 minutes.

3. Remove the saucepan from the heat. Let cool slightly, then transfer mixture to a blender along with the blanched vegetables and cream. Puree until smooth. Season to taste with salt and pepper. It will need a good dose of salt, since nothing has been seasoned yet.

4. Chill the vichyssoise for at least 3 hours or, better still, overnight to allow the flavors to develop. Once it's cold you will need to adjust seasoning again by adding more salt. It's best served as cold as possible. It will keep for several days; just stir well before serving.

Matzo Balls

Matzo balls (aka *kneidlach*) are the iconic Jewish recipe. People may not know a single Jew or a single thing about Judaism, but they will know what matzo balls look and taste like. And they usually want to know a little more about the Jewish culture once they've tried them (they're that delicious). These are fluffy and flavorful, spiked with fresh parsley. I could be overselling them, but you may want to convert, is all I'm saying.

4 eggs, beaten

1 cup matzo meal

2 Tbsp vegetable oil

2 tsp sea salt

¼ tsp pepper

2 Tbsp finely chopped flat-leaf parsley

1 tsp baking powder

¼ cup soda water

1. In a large bowl, stir together the eggs, matzo meal, oil, salt, pepper, parsley and baking powder. Add the soda water and use a rubber spatula to mix well. Cover with plastic wrap and refrigerate for 1 hour.

2. Bring a large pot of salted water to a boil, then lower heat to a simmer. With wet or oiled hands, gently form the matzo mix into golf ball-size balls, dropping them into the water as you go. When all of the matzo balls are formed and cooking, cover the pot and gently simmer for 35–40 minutes, or until cooked through and soft.

3. Remove from the liquid with a slotted spoon and serve in chicken soup. You can also make them 1 day in advance and keep them covered in the fridge, warming them up in the soup.

Split Pea & Noodle Soup

At over 100 years young, United Bakers Dairy Restaurant in Toronto is the place to go when you want to see everyone you went to Young Judea camps with. Just like the people, the food never changes, and that's a good thing. They make the best soups, including a pea soup with noodles that is nourishing comfort in a bowl. This is my take on it.

1 Tbsp olive oil

1 medium onion, chopped

2 cloves garlic, finely chopped

6 cups vegetable or chicken stock (see note)

1 cup dried green split peas, picked through and rinsed

1 large carrot, peeled and chopped

1 bay leaf

Sea salt and pepper to taste

1 cup dried spaghetti, broken into 2-inch pieces

¼ cup chopped dill

1. Place the oil in a large stockpot. Add the onions and sauté for about 5 minutes, until golden. Add the garlic, stir for 1 minute, then add the stock, split peas, carrots, bay leaf, salt and pepper. Bring to a boil, then lower heat to a simmer and cook, covered, for 1½ hours.

2. Remove the bay leaf, let the soup cool slightly, then puree in batches in a blender or in the pot with an immersion blender. Place the soup back on the heat and stir in the spaghetti. Bring to a boil, then lower heat to a simmer and cook, uncovered, for another 10–12 minutes, until noodles are al dente. Remove from the heat and stir in the dill. Serve hot.

Note: If you use chicken stock, this recipe will no longer qualify as pareve.

Roasted Butternut Squash Soup

Every now and then when I'd join my friend Natasha's family for dinner at her parent's house, I was amazed by the large tables full of friendly familiar and unfamiliar faces—Anita and Cyril had a wonderful open-door policy, and still do. The other thing that struck me was that, because Natasha and some of her siblings were vegetarian (and still are), a pureed vegetable soup with a matzo ball was always offered in addition to the traditional chicken soup—yet another sign of their inclusiveness. Also, matzo balls in butternut squash soup taste amazing.

1 (2–3 lb) butternut squash

1 large onion, coarsely chopped

1 large carrot, peeled and sliced into ½-inch pieces

6 cups vegetable or chicken stock (see note on page 65)

Sea salt and pepper to taste

2 Tbsp finely chopped sage

½ cup apple butter, for garnish (optional)

1. Preheat the oven to 350°F and oil a baking sheet.

2. Cut the butternut squash in half and remove the seeds with a large spoon. Place the squash cut side down on the baking sheet and bake for 40–50 minutes, or until the flesh of the squash is very soft. Remove from the oven and let cool. Once cool, scrape the flesh from the skin and place it in a bowl. Discard the skin.

3. Place the squash, onions, carrots, stock, salt and pepper in a medium pot and simmer for 35–40 minutes. Remove from the heat and let cool for 15 minutes. Puree in a blender on high speed in small batches, until all of the soup is blended and smooth, or save yourself the cleanup and do it in the pot with an immersion blender. It won't be quite as smooth, but it will still be delightful.

4. Reheat the soup, add the sage and season with more salt and pepper to taste. If you like, serve with a dollop of apple butter.

Chicken Soup (aka Jewish Penicillin)

SERVES

10–12

A bowl of matzo ball soup is like Jewish echinacea. In fact, do a double-blind taste test and I think you'll find this golden broth goes a long way to healing what ails you, heart and soul. (But especially soul.)

1 roasting chicken, giblet bag removed, trimmed of excess fat and rinsed

2 parsnips, peeled and ends chopped off

2 stalks celery with leaves

2 large onions, halved

6 medium carrots, peeled and ends chopped off

1 Tbsp sea salt, plus more to taste

Pepper to taste

1 small bunch flat-leaf parsley

¼ cup chopped dill, plus a few sprigs for garnish

1. Put the chicken in a very large pot and pour in about 12–14 cups water, making sure clucky is covered. With the stockpot uncovered, bring to a boil, using a slotted spoon to skim and discard the foam that accumulates. Reduce the heat to a simmer and add the whole parsnips, celery, onions and carrots and the salt and pepper. Cook, partially covered, for at least 2 hours (3 hours is better, though). Skim occasionally as foam appears. With about 10 minutes to go, toss in the parsley and dill.

2. For a pristine broth, remove the chicken, veggies and herbs from the pot and set aside. Strain the soup through a sieve or colander lined with cheesecloth (or a double layer of paper towel), returning the clear broth to a clean pot. Shred or slice the chicken; discard the onions, celery and parsley; and roughly chop the carrots and parsnips and add them back into the soup before serving.

3. To serve, spoon a ladle or two of broth, then add a few pieces of carrot, parsnip, a *bisl* of chicken (use the rest for chicken salad sandwiches tomorrow) and a sprig of fresh dill into each bowl. This is even better bejeweled with a couple of matzo balls (p. 64), meat *kreplach* (p. 60) or egg noodles (p. 70). Shabbat shalom.

Passover Soup Noodles

These simple egg noodles are as delicate as a cloud and are a great change-up from *kneidlach* (aka matzo balls) once you get into the waning days of Passover.

6 room-temperature eggs, beaten

½ cup water, room temperature

¼ cup potato starch

½ tsp sea salt

1. Combine the eggs and water in a bowl, then whisk in the potato starch and salt until well blended.

2. Heat a large nonstick pan over medium heat. Ladle in about ¼ cup batter and roll around like a crepe until the pan is evenly covered. Set the pan back on the heat until the top seems dry, about 1–2 minutes. Then, using a small rubber spatula, roll the crepe into a little cigar and slice into ¼-inch circles. Unroll and separate so they look like noodles. Repeat with the remaining batter, stirring between crepes to make sure the potato starch hasn't settled, until all the batter is used up. You should make about 10 crepes.

3. Add the noodles to bowls and ladle hot chicken soup overtop. The noodles can be made in advance and stored in an airtight container in the fridge for up to 3 days.

Cold Beet Borscht

It's hot and cool. It's sweet and sour. As a kid, you obviously had to be forced to eat something as insanely unappealing as beet soup, but as you grew a little older you were able to cut up the hot potato in the soup with the spoon by yourself, then swirl in that sour cream as you saw fit. Not only did you realize that deep purple plus creamy white makes a pretty raspberry pink, but also that bubbes make the best soup ever.

2 Tbsp olive oil	1 medium carrot, peeled and diced	3 Tbsp sugar
1 large onion, diced		Sea salt and pepper to taste
3 large roasted beets, diced (see note)	1 stalk celery, diced	3 medium Yukon Gold potatoes
	4 cups vegetable stock	
2 large field tomatoes, diced	4 Tbsp red wine vinegar	Sour cream and dill, for garnish

1. Heat the oil in a stockpot over medium heat, then add the onions and cook until soft, about 4–6 minutes. Add the beets, tomatoes, carrots and celery, and cook for 2–3 minutes more. Add the stock, vinegar, sugar and salt and pepper. Taste and adjust for that perfect sweet-and-sour balance. You may need to add more vinegar or sugar to achieve this. Trust your taste buds. Bring to a boil, then lower the heat to a simmer and cook for about 30 minutes, or until the vegetables are tender.

2. Cool the soup and refrigerate overnight. The day you plan to serve the soup, make the potatoes. Bring a large pot of salted water to a boil, add the whole potatoes and lower the heat to a simmer. Cover the pot and boil for 20–25 minutes, or until the potatoes are cooked through. Peel while hot, slice in half and place in a medium serving bowl.

3. To serve, ladle the cold soup into bowls, then pass around the hot potatoes, sour cream and some fresh dill for garnish.

Note: To roast the beets, preheat the oven to 425°F. Wash and trim the beets and wrap them tightly in foil. Roast in the oven for about 1 hour, or until a knife slides in with little to no resistance. Peel the beets over the sink and proceed with the recipe.

Chapter 3

NOSHES & SIDES

(Pareve & Dairy)

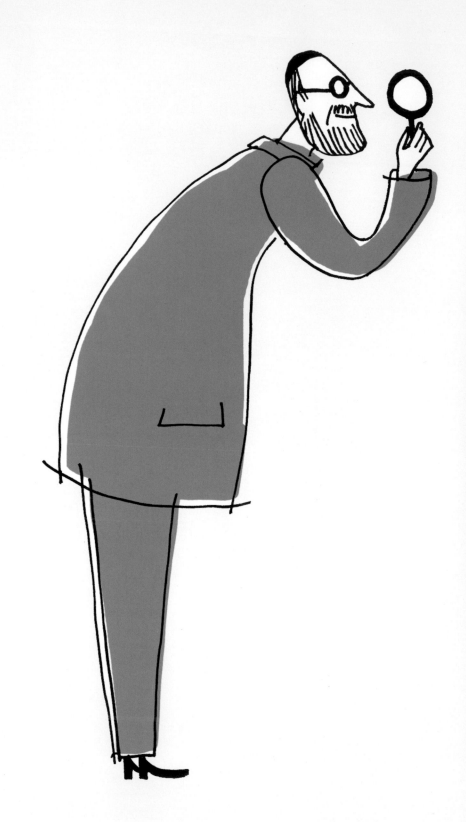

Kosher Quality

"Over-Gefilte-Fishing Sparks Greenpeace Cry for Gefilte-Fishing Moratorium" is the fairly hilarious headline on a fake news story I read recently, the joke being that gefilte fish is not a fish but in fact a traditional Jewish "delicacy" fashioned from chopped pickled carp covered in aspic and studded with boiled carrot. (Think of it as a cod cake in a *yarmulke*.) I recall this joke on a sunny spring afternoon as I drive toward Fair Haven, Newfoundland, where everywhere I look there's nothing but marble-blue ponds and rolling hills that will eventually tumble into the Atlantic Ocean. I remember this joke because not only am I driving through the land of fish moratoriums, but I'm also headed toward Neptune Sea Products—Atlantic Canada's only kosher-sanctioned secondary fish-processing plant, with a pit stop at the country's only kosher winery.

Here in cod's land, Bond Rideout Jr. leads me on a tour of his kosher processing plant, with gleaming white walls, concrete floors, high ceilings and stainless-steel everything else. I see hundreds of capelin, the tiny iridescent fish that start rolling into nearby coves during springtime, smoked and resting on racks.

"There's no question that kosher is growing," Rabbi Chaim Goldberg tells me over the phone from New York, in a voice that's a cross between Jackie Mason and my cousin Irv. Goldberg is a Rabbinic coordinator at the nonprofit Orthodox Union (OU), the authority that, among other things, stages surprise inspections of kosher-certified institutions to make sure that everything's, well, kosher. "As the world is getting more global, manufacturers in places that have never seen a Jew before, and may never see a Jew, see kosher as a very easy way to market their product."

Typically, people have their own ideas of what kosher means, with "healthy," "clean" and "pure" being common descriptors. While the A-OK from a *mashgiach*—the specially trained kosher inspector—has more to do with complex Talmudic and biblical laws than idyllic coastal scenes, even the nonobservant perceive the COR or OU symbol as a standard of excellence.

It's a multi-billion-a-year business in North America, say the reps at Manischewitz, the king of the kosher brands. And New-foundland's Neptune has secured a *bisl* of that *kashrut* pie by producing some 200

different products, from wasabi salmon to Cajun cod.

Local fishermen bring in all the codfish, mackerel and herring. Smoked salmon—cold-smoked on-site in one of six large smoker rooms using a secret 400-year-old recipe from the Isle of Man—is the bestseller. "We only use fish that have fins and scales," Rideout explains. "The other main thing is, my employees can't bring in ham sandwiches for lunch."

Danny Bath, a former fisherman who does research and development for Neptune, has created a line of spreads that he'd like me to try. The cream-cheese-based schmears are reminiscent of every happy Jewish brunch table I've ever noshed at, all smooth and creamy with an intoxicating natural wood-smoke finish. I almost single-handedly polish off two tubs, yet still want more. Products this good cross religious and cultural lines.

After leaving the plant, I drive about 15 minutes down a rural road to the Rodrigues Winery in Markland, where Hilary and Marie-France Rodrigues rolled out their first batch of fruit wine in 1993. This being Newfoundland's first winery (and a couple of decades later, the first commercially operating distillery in the province), the government ended up applying the same regulations as for a dairy: you couldn't put milk in barrels, so you couldn't put wine in barrels. In the end, the nonsensical rules that had forced the Rodrigueses to ferment their fruit wines in stainless-steel, double-lined milk tanks made it easier to be kosher, as part of the process involves letting water boil in the tanks for a certain amount of time. The result: a tasty niche product and the only kosher and sulfite-free winery in Canada.

Rodrigues Winery now produces over 12,000 cases a year, and its bottles are found on wine lists in restaurants from St. John's to Japan. Made from handpicked fruit, the kosher quaffs come in a dozen varieties, including local blueberries, cranberries and indigenous cloudberries harvested from creeping plants found on the northern peat bogs of Newfoundland and Labrador.

The Rodrigueses' son, Lionel, leads me through a wine tasting. The blackcurrant wine tastes of pure local blackcurrants. The strawberry reminds me of the real thing—like juicy summer strawberries, not strawberry candy. Lionel says they've also held wine tastings at the Beth El Synagogue in St. John's, but when I ask if he's heard that old joke about Jews not being big drinkers, he looks puzzled.

"Really?" he says. "At the temple tastings they seem to drink." Then he takes another thoughtful sip of his kosher blueberry wine and concludes, "But then again, we're all Newfoundlanders."

Honey-Harissa Roasted Carrots

I used to dread carrot *tzimmes* during the holidays (think: mushy carrots sweetened with honey and sprinkled with plump raisins or prunes). It was my idea of hell in vegetable side-dish form. What doesn't kill you makes you stronger, so I've created a hot new take on this High Holidays dish—which, ironically, was meant to symbolize a sweet New Year. Spicy, sweet, juicy and crunchy: these carrots are nothing short of heavenly.

12 medium carrots, trimmed and peeled

1 Tbsp olive oil

Kosher salt to taste

1 Tbsp honey

1 tsp harissa

2 green onions, trimmed and thinly sliced

Seeds from ½ pomegranate (about ½ cup)

¼ cup shelled pistachios, roughly chopped

1. Preheat the oven to 425°F and line a baking sheet with parchment paper.

2. Scatter the carrots on the baking sheet so they're evenly spaced and not crowding the pan. Drizzle with olive oil and season with salt. Combine the honey and harissa in a small bowl, then drizzle over the carrots. Roast in the preheated oven for 30 minutes, or until cooked through and slightly browned, shaking the baking sheet once or twice during cooking.

3. When the carrots are done, transfer to a serving dish. Let cool slightly, then sprinkle with the green onions, pomegranate seeds and pistachios. Serve warm or at room temperature.

Sour Cream & Onion Potato Knishes

I *like* knishes but I don't *love* knishes. I always liked the flaky pastry, but found the fillings to be a little meh. So I thought, what if I added sour cream and green onions, turning meh into mmm? These knishes happily live at the intersection of loaded baked potato and Saturday-morning bat mitzvah lessons.

FOR THE DOUGH:

2½ cups flour

1 tsp baking powder

½ tsp sea salt

1 egg

½ cup olive oil

1 tsp white vinegar

½ cup water

FOR THE FILLING:

3 medium Yukon Gold potatoes, peeled and halved

2 Tbsp butter

¼ cup full-fat sour cream

4 green onions, trimmed and thinly sliced

1 egg, beaten

Sea salt and pepper to taste

1 egg, beaten, for egg wash

Pinch of sesame seeds

1. To make the dough, stir together the flour, baking powder and salt in a medium bowl. In a small bowl, whisk together the egg, oil, vinegar and water. Pour the egg mixture into the dry ingredients and stir until it starts to come together. Then tip out onto a lightly floured surface and knead for 1–2 minutes, until the dough is smooth. Clean the bowl, then place the dough back in the bowl and cover with a tea towel. Set aside for 1 hour in a warm, draft-free place.

2. To make the filling, boil the potatoes in salted boiling water until tender, about 25 minutes. Drain and mash the potatoes in the pot, along with the butter, sour cream, green onions, beaten egg, salt and pepper. Set aside to cool completely.

3. Preheat the oven to 350°F and line a baking sheet with parchment paper.

4. On a floured surface, roll the dough out into a large rectangle, as thinly as possible, about ⅛ inch thick. Then cut into 3-inch rounds (you can use the top of a water glass for this if you don't have a cookie cutter). Stretch the rounds out a bit, then place

1 tablespoon of the cooled potato filling in the middle of each round. Pull the dough up around the filling and pinch the edges closed at the top. You should have about 15 small knishes at the end.

5. Place the knishes on the prepared baking sheet and brush with egg wash. Sprinkle with a pinch of sesame seeds. Bake in the preheated oven for 25–30 minutes, or until golden brown.

Crispy Smashed Baby Potatoes with Malt Vinegar

I'm a Jew, but I'm also a Canadian, so I was weaned on salt and vinegar potato chips, a hangover from the days when we were ruled by the British Empire. As a Canadian Jewess, I carry my flavor memories with me wherever I may roam (especially since I never stopped cramming my face with salt and vinegar chips). Herewith, I present crispy roasted potatoes with the flavors of the Commonwealth. Long may they reign!

1½ lb baby potatoes

½ cup olive oil

2 tsp kosher salt

½ tsp pepper

Malt vinegar to taste (optional)

1. Preheat the oven to 450°F.

2. Bring a medium pot of water to a boil. Add the potatoes, and when the water boils again, set a timer for 10 minutes. The potatoes should be slightly soft. If they're not soft enough, cook for another 2–5 minutes, then drain in a colander.

3. Spread a tea towel over a rimmed baking sheet, and pour the drained potatoes over the towel. Pat to dry, remove the towel and, using the back of a fork, gently press down on the potatoes until the skins break and the potatoes flatten slightly.

4. Pour the oil overtop, toss to coat and season with the salt and pepper. Bake in the preheated oven for 40 minutes, then flip the potatoes and bake for another 10–15 minutes, until browned and crispy. Season with malt vinegar, if using, when potatoes are hot from the oven.

Gefilte Fish Loaf

I'm not on board with grinding and poaching whitefish for hours and chilling it in its collagen-heavy fish stock. That's why jarred gefilte fish is such big business. However, this easy take on gefilte fish features fresh fish, a quick bake and slicing *sans* fish jelly. It's a slightly sweet and salty tradition, minus the stinky house.

2 large carrots

2 onions

2 lb boneless, skinless whitefish fillets such as carp, pollock or pike

4 Tbsp sugar

1 tsp pepper

2 tsp sea salt

1 cup matzo meal

3 eggs

1 head leaf lettuce, for serving

Jarred beet horseradish, for serving

Curly parsley, for garnish

1. Preheat the oven to 350°F and grease a 9 × 5-inch loaf pan with vegetable oil.

2. In a food processor, finely grind the carrots and onions. Transfer the vegetables to a large bowl. Place the fish in the food processor and pulse until finely chopped. Add the fish to the vegetables, then add the sugar, pepper, salt, matzo meal and eggs. Mix well, then spoon into the prepared loaf pan, pressing down firmly with the back of a spatula and smoothing out the top.

3. Bake for 1 hour. Remove the loaf from the oven and run a knife around the edges to be sure it's not sticking to the pan. Refrigerate for at least 4 hours, but it's best to leave overnight.

4. When ready to serve, remove the loaf from the pan. Slice and serve cold on a nice piece of leaf lettuce with a dollop of spicy horseradish and a sprig of parsley.

Hummus with Zhug

A Middle Eastern masterpiece gets a Yemeni upgrade with zhug, a cilantro-based hot sauce. A gift to the masses spread over pita or dipped with crudités, hummus is healthy, delicious and full of flavor. If you think about it, it's like the new peanut butter. By the way, these two recipes are great together, but also apart. Hummus topped with cooked ground lamb and pine nuts is a hearty main, while zhug can be a delightful marinade for meat and fish or used to add punch to shakshuka or grilled vegetables.

FOR THE HUMMUS:

1 clove garlic, crushed

½ tsp sea salt

½ tsp cumin seeds

1 (19 oz) can chickpeas, drained and rinsed

2 Tbsp tahini, well stirred

¼ cup olive oil

¼ cup water

Juice of ½ lemon

FOR THE ZHUG:

1 cup chopped cilantro

1 cup chopped flat-leaf parsley

4 jalapeños (seeds and veins removed if you want it less spicy), chopped

3 cloves garlic, peeled

Juice of ½ lemon

2 Tbsp olive oil

½ tsp ground cumin

1 tsp ground coriander

Sea salt and pepper to taste

Pita bread, for serving

1. To make the hummus, place the garlic, salt, cumin seeds and chickpeas in a food processor and puree. Add the tahini and blend. With the food processor running, slowly stream in the oil and then the water, until the hummus gets that hummusy texture. Add more water if needed. Next add the lemon juice. Taste for seasoning and adjust if needed. Blend once more, then transfer to an airtight container and place in the fridge to allow it to firm up a bit.

2. For the zhug, place the cilantro, parsley, jalapeños, garlic, lemon juice, olive oil, cumin, coriander and salt and pepper in a food processor and blend until smooth. Serve spooned beside or over the hummus, with pita bread for ripping and dipping. Store any extra in an airtight container in the fridge for up to 1 week.

Skillet Kugel

6–8

Kugel was never my favorite. It was often dry from too much cottage cheese or greasy from too much oil. The noodles were undercooked and hard, then overbaked to become even harder. Sometimes it was made sweet with raisins and sugar, sometimes it was made savory with salt and pepper, but it was always leaden. However, it's a quintessential Jewish food, so I couldn't write this book without including a great kugel recipe. I've upped the luxurious dairy, added cinnamon and a crunchy cornflake topper, and baked it in a skillet. Let's make new memories with this tasty kugel!

3 eggs

¾ cup full-fat cottage cheese

½ cup full-fat sour cream

⅓ cup brown sugar

1 cup milk

3 Tbsp butter, melted, plus extra for greasing

1 tsp vanilla extract

½ tsp salt

1 (12 oz) bag broad egg noodles

FOR THE TOPPING:

½ cup coarsely crushed cornflakes

1 Tbsp butter, melted

2 Tbsp brown sugar

1 tsp ground cinnamon

Pinch of sea salt

1. In a food processor fitted with the metal blade, whirl together the eggs, cottage cheese, sour cream, brown sugar, milk, melted butter, vanilla and salt.

2. Grease a large cast-iron skillet and set aside. Bring a large pot of salted water to a boil and cook the noodles until al dente, about 5 minutes (but check the package directions). Drain the noodles and add back to the empty pot. Stir in the egg-cheese mixture, then pour into the skillet. Set aside for 10 minutes.

3. Preheat the oven to 350°F.

4. To make the topping, toss together the cornflakes, melted butter, brown sugar, cinnamon and salt in a small bowl. Sprinkle the topping overtop the kugel. Bake for 35–40 minutes, or until lightly browned. Let stand for at least 10 minutes before serving.

Beets with Balsamic–Pistachio Brittle

What do beets with brittle have to do with being Jewish? Think *shtetl*. Think borscht. Think sweet and sour, earthiness and effort. Now think of how far we've come. So now you also get goat cheese and fancy brittle. (Pistachios too.)

5–6 medium beets (about 2 lb), trimmed of stems and roots

2 Tbsp plus 2 tsp balsamic vinegar, divided

Finishing salt (such as Maldon)

¼ cup shelled pistachios

½ cup sugar

5 oz soft goat cheese

1–2 Tbsp extra virgin olive oil

2 tsp thyme leaves

1. Preheat the oven to 425°F.

2. Scrub and dry the trimmed beets, then wrap in foil and place on a baking sheet. Roast for 60–80 minutes, or until just tender. Unwrap, let cool, then remove the skins (they should slide right off). Cut the beets into wedges and toss with 2 tablespoons balsamic.

3. Line a baking sheet with parchment paper. Sprinkle with a pinch of finishing salt and the pistachios, making a large rectangle on the paper.

4. Place the sugar in a large nonstick skillet over medium-low heat, and cook until the sugar is totally melted. Don't stir the sugar, but it's okay to swirl the pan now and then for even cooking. Add the remaining 2 teaspoons balsamic and swirl the pan around until the sugar is totally melted again and has started to caramelize. Evenly pour the mixture over the nuts and salt, then wiggle the pan so the caramel spreads and forms an even layer. Let cool for 10 minutes, then break into small shards.

5. Arrange the beet wedges on a serving platter. Break the goat cheese into walnut-size chunks and scatter them here and there over and around the beets. Drizzle beets and cheese with olive oil and a pinch more of finishing salt. Tuck the pistachio shards into the arrangement and sprinkle all with fresh thyme.

Super-Crunchy Onion Rings

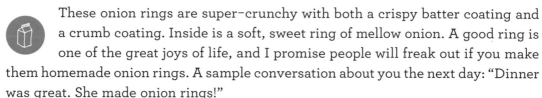

These onion rings are super-crunchy with both a crispy batter coating and a crumb coating. Inside is a soft, sweet ring of mellow onion. A good ring is one of the great joys of life, and I promise people will freak out if you make them homemade onion rings. A sample conversation about you the next day: "Dinner was great. She made onion rings!"

2 large sweet onions (such as Vidalia), cut into ¼-inch rings

3 cups flour

1 tsp baking powder

1 tsp sea salt

2 cups vegetable oil

2 cups panko breadcrumbs

2 eggs, beaten

2 cups buttermilk

Seasoned salt (such as Lawry's) to taste

1. Separate the onions into the individual rings, discarding the cores, and set aside. In a medium bowl, stir together the flour, baking powder and salt.

2. In a large, deep skillet, heat the oil to 365°F.

3. While the oil is heating, dip the onion rings into the flour mixture until they are all coated. Set aside on a wire rack.

4. Pour the panko crumbs into a medium bowl.

5. In another medium bowl, whisk the eggs and buttermilk together, then add to the flour mixture, stirring gently until combined. Dip the floured rings into the batter to coat, then shake off any excess and toss in panko crumbs to coat. Repeat with all the rings.

6. Deep-fry the rings, four or five at a time, for 2-3 minutes, or until golden brown and crunchy, flipping them midway through cooking. Transfer the rings to a plate lined with paper towel to drain. Sprinkle generously with seasoned salt and serve at once.

The Best Caesar Salad

Jewish women love Caesar salads as much as Jewish men love French onion soup. Or at least that's the way it was when I was growing up in Toronto in the heady 1980s. We troublesome teens would all go for late-night noshes at Toby's Good Eats, where the flirting and gossip were almost as delicious as the pub grub. Some things should never change.

FOR THE CROUTONS:

2 Tbsp olive oil

1 clove garlic, smashed

5 slices baguette, cut into ½-inch cubes

Pinch of sea salt

FOR THE DRESSING:

2 cloves garlic, finely chopped

1 egg yolk

¼ tsp sea salt, plus extra to taste

1 tsp Worcestershire sauce

1 tsp anchovy paste

¼ tsp pepper

¼ tsp sugar

¼ tsp dry mustard

Juice of ½ lemon

⅓ cup extra virgin olive oil

1 large head romaine lettuce, washed, dried and torn into bite-size pieces

½ cup freshly grated or shaved Parmigiano-Reggiano

1. To make the croutons, heat the olive oil in a large nonstick skillet over medium heat. Add the smashed garlic and cook until golden. Trash the garlic, then add the bread cubes, stirring to coat with the oil. Get them good and toasty, 2–3 minutes, then remove from the heat and add a pinch of salt. No noshing.

2. To make the dressing, get out the blender (or a whisk and bowl or a jar with a lid) and mix together the two finely chopped cloves of garlic with the egg yolk, salt, Worcestershire sauce, anchovy paste, pepper, sugar, dry mustard and lemon juice. Gradually drizzle in the oil. Blend until combined. Taste for seasoning and adjust as needed. This is best made at least a few hours in advance to allow the flavors to meld.

3. Place the torn head of lettuce in a large bowl, toss with dressing to coat and add the croutons from the pan, and the Parmigiano-Reggiano. Toss it up and dish it out. Add grilled chicken or fish for a nice lunch—$7 extra charge.

Lacy Latkes & Applesauce

Humble and comforting, sexy and ready to party, potato latkes are the greatest singular recipe in the Jewish repertoire. They define Chanukah. They are a deli mainstay. They can swing from dairy to pareve with a dollop of sour cream or a splash of applesauce. They can even be highfalutin when topped with caviar for a fancy *simcha*. They are as traditional as recipes come, yet are also a path to the future.

8 large Russet potatoes, scrubbed clean	Sea salt and pepper to taste (be generous)
2 onions, finely chopped	Vegetable oil, for frying
3 eggs, beaten	Homemade applesauce (recipe follows), sour cream or Greek yogurt, for garnish (see note)
⅓ cup flour or matzo meal	

1. Using a food processor or box grater, grate the potatoes (no need to peel them). Transfer the potatoes to a clean tea towel or cheesecloth and squeeze out the potato liquid, getting the shreds as dry as possible.

2. Place the potatoes in a very large bowl and mix together with the chopped onions, eggs, flour, salt and pepper. The acid in the onions will stop the potatoes from browning.

3. In a large cast-iron skillet (or other heavy-bottomed skillet), heat ½ inch of oil over medium heat. Add heaping tablespoons of latke mixture, frying four or five at a time, for about 3 minutes on each side, or until golden brown. Smoosh them down with the spatula a bit and add more oil as needed.

4. When the latkes are cooked, transfer them to a plate lined with paper towel to drain. You can serve these immediately or cook them ahead and reheat in the oven when guests arrive. Serve with applesauce, sour cream or Greek yogurt.

Note: If you garnish with sour cream or yogurt, this recipe will become dairy.

(continued)

Homemade Applesauce

MAKES ABOUT 2 CUPS

2 lb McIntosh apples (about 6 medium),
peeled, cored and chopped

Juice of 1 lemon

2 Tbsp brown sugar

½ tsp ground cinnamon

Pinch of sea salt

½ cup water

1. In a medium pot, bring the apples, lemon juice, sugar, cinnamon, salt and water to a boil. Lower heat to a simmer, stirring often, until the apples are cooked and start falling apart, about 15 minutes. Blitz in the pot with an immersion blender until the desired consistency is achieved. Serve with latkes.

The Big Salad

SERVES

4–6

This recipe is an ode to what I'd imagine Elaine's controversial mid-1990s *Seinfeld* salad would include. I'm thinking tons of stuff, then more stuff, plus an old-school homemade Italian dressing and some croutons. This is a starting point. Dress yours up or dress it down. But whatever you do, please acknowledge who paid for the big salad.

FOR THE DRESSING:

1 clove garlic, finely chopped

1 Tbsp smooth Dijon mustard

1 Tbsp honey

¼ cup red wine vinegar

1 tsp dried oregano

½ tsp red pepper flakes

¼ cup freshly grated Parmigiano-Reggiano

¼ cup extra virgin olive oil

FOR THE CROUTONS:

2 Tbsp olive oil

5 slices baguette, cut into cubes or torn into bite-size pieces

Sea salt to taste

FOR THE SALAD:

2 eggs

1 large head romaine lettuce, washed, dried and torn into bite-size pieces

1 red pepper, seeded and sliced

1 large carrot, roughly grated

½ English cucumber, cut into half-moons

4–5 red radishes, thinly sliced

6–8 button mushrooms, thinly sliced

2 large tomatoes, sliced into wedges

1. For the dressing, whisk together the garlic, Dijon, honey, vinegar, oregano, red pepper flakes and Parmigiano-Reggiano. Slowly drizzle in the olive oil, whisking until emulsified. This makes about 1 cup, and you can store any extra in an airtight container for up to 2 weeks.

2. To make the croutons, heat the olive oil in a large nonstick skillet over medium heat. Add the bread cubes, stirring to coat them with the oil. Get them good and toasty, 2–3 minutes. Remove from the heat and add salt to taste.

(continued)

3. Bring a small pot of water to a boil and add the 2 eggs. Reduce to a simmer and cook for 12 minutes. Rinse the eggs under cold water, then peel and slice the eggs in half.

4. Get out a big salad bowl for your big salad. Place the prepared romaine, red peppers, carrots, cucumbers, radishes, mushrooms and tomatoes in the bowl. Toss with the dressing to taste (but don't drown it), then sprinkle with croutons from the pan and put an egg half in each quadrant of the bowl. Serve at once.

Orange & Carrot Salad

Ribbons of orange on orange with a hint of honey, a burst of mint and the toasty crunch of pine nuts make this simple salad a take-notice side dish. It's a reminder that a few simple ingredients can come together to make a greater whole, while making you look like a real *balabusta*.

4 large carrots

4 large seedless navel oranges

¼ cup pine nuts

Juice of 1 lemon

1 Tbsp honey

¼ red onion, thinly sliced

½ cup mint leaves

Sea salt to taste

Pinch of red pepper flakes

1. Peel the carrots, then using the same peeler, make ribbons out of the carrots, peeling away until you get down to the woody core. Discard woody carrot cores or eat them as a cook's snack.

2. Cut the tops and bottoms off the oranges. Cutting vertically, slice the peel off, then cut out the segments between the membranes. You'll wind up with orange supremes.

3. Lightly toast the pine nuts in a dry pan over medium heat. Keep an eye on them, as they burn easily.

4. Mix the lemon juice and honey in your serving bowl. Add the carrot ribbons, oranges and red onions, then gently toss with dressing. Tear up the mint leaves, add to the salad and toss once more. Scatter the toasted pine nuts overtop and sprinkle with a pinch of salt and red pepper flakes. Toss once more and serve.

Greek Orzo Salad

This is the perfect salad for those summertime days when you've got drop-by guests and don't want to do much cooking. Just boil some orzo, chop up some veggies, grill some corn and scoop some ice cream for dessert. It'll be a perfect, lazy afternoon.

1 cup dried orzo pasta

1 clove garlic

Pinch of sea salt

Juice of 1 small lemon

¼ cup olive oil

6–8 cups baby spinach

2 Tbsp cold water

¼ cup pine nuts

1 handful mint leaves, chopped

½ English cucumber, chopped

¼ cup kalamata olives, pitted and chopped

1 (19 oz) can chickpeas, drained and rinsed

½ cup crumbled feta cheese

Pinch of red pepper flakes

Sea salt and pepper to taste

1. Bring a medium pot of salted water to a boil. Cook the orzo following the package directions, about 8–10 minutes. Drain well, then transfer to a serving bowl and pop into the fridge to cool.

2. To make the dressing, finely chop the garlic with a pinch of sea salt, then whisk together with the lemon juice and olive oil. Add the dressing to the orzo and gently toss.

3. Rinse out the orzo cooking pot and add the spinach and 2 tablespoons cold water. Cook for 2–3 minutes, or until wilted, then puree with an immersion blender in the pot or in a food processor until the spinach is smooth. Add to the orzo bowl.

4. Lightly toast the pine nuts in a small, dry skillet over medium heat (watch them closely—they burn easily). Add the toasted pine nuts, mint, cucumber, olives, chickpeas, feta and red pepper flakes to the orzo and gently toss. Taste for seasoning and adjust if needed. Chill for at least 3 hours before serving.

Kasha Pilaf

This is a 21st-century Semitic pilaf for a generation of kasha haters. What's kasha? It's a grain—buckwheat groats to be exact; a traditional Jewish dish that my three brothers and I loathed. My oldest brother, David, said it was impossible to make people like kasha. I think it was the mushy bowtie pasta and neon yellow soup base we grew up on. But during a recent Rosh Hashanah, I made it my mission to turn it tasty, adding kale, nuts, dill, onion and meaty mushrooms to the mix. Before the night was over, David had secretly texted many family members to get their votes. He liked it, and so did everyone else. My dad said, "I can't get excited about kasha because it's kasha. But I will say it's the best kasha I've had." And that, my friends, is considered a win in the Rosen family.

4 cups vegetable stock

2 cups kasha

1 small bunch kale, fibrous veins removed

1 cup walnut pieces

1 Tbsp olive oil

1 small red onion, thinly sliced

4 cups stemmed and quartered button mushrooms

¼ cup chopped dill

Juice of 1 lemon

Sea salt and pepper to taste

1 tsp honey

1. In a medium pot, bring the vegetable stock to a boil, then add the kasha. Bring back to a boil, then reduce to a simmer for 10 minutes, or until cooked. Fluff the kasha with a fork, then tip into a large bowl to cool.

2. Rinse the pot and add about 1 cup of water. Bring to a boil, then lower heat to a simmer and add the kale. Cover with a lid and steam for 8–10 minutes, or until tender. Drain and chop the kale and add to the big kasha bowl. Wipe out the pot (can you tell I hate doing dishes?) and toast the walnut pieces over medium heat for 3–4 minutes, or until slightly browned. Add them to the kasha.

3. Drizzle the olive oil into the pot and sauté the red onions over medium heat for 5 minutes, then add the quartered mushrooms and cook for about 15 minutes more. Add to the kasha, along with the chopped dill, lemon juice, salt, pepper and honey. Serve warm for a hearty and healthy New Year.

Israeli Salad & Homemade Labneh

When my late Uncle Michael met a young Israeli woman and married her, we got not only Auntie Irit in the deal but also her recipe for my favorite salad of all time. From breakfast to dinner, this simple salad is as fresh and cool as my amazing aunt.

FOR THE LABNEH:

3 cups 2% plain yogurt

½ tsp sea salt

1 tsp lemon zest

FOR THE SALAD:

3 large juicy tomatoes, diced

1 English cucumber, seeded and diced

¼ large sweet onion, diced

Juice of 2 lemons

½ tsp sea salt

¼ tsp pepper

Pinch of sugar

Pita bread, for serving

1. To make the labneh, combine the yogurt and salt and mix well. Line a medium bowl with a piece of cheesecloth that has been folded over once for thickness. Place the yogurt mixture in the middle of the cheesecloth. Carefully bring up the sides of the cheesecloth around the yogurt, making a leak-free pouch. Tie up the ends of the cheesecloth with string or a twist-tie, then hang off of a wooden spoon balanced over the bowl. Refrigerate for 24 hours—the bowl will catch the whey. You can also tie the cheesecloth pouch right to a rack in the fridge and place a bowl on the shelf beneath to catch the whey. After 24 hours, mix the lemon zest into the drained yogurt, discarding the whey. Refrigerate until ready to use.

2. For the salad, place the tomatoes, cucumbers, onions, lemon juice, salt, pepper and sugar in a large bowl. Stir to combine. Serve the salad alongside a big dollop of labneh and pita bread for ripping and dipping.

Bibb Lettuce with Root Chips

This salad has the fresh crispness of lettuce and the deeper crunch of fried root chips. It's kind of what Archie and Jughead are to health food and junk food—what you should eat and what you want to eat, all at once. But which one's which? (Wait a minute, are we still talking about this delicious salad or have I moved on to *Riverdale*?) I guess that makes Veronica the zippy vinaigrette. (*Riverdale* it is! What is even happening?)

⅓ cup extra virgin olive oil

Juice of 1 lemon

1 clove garlic, finely chopped

1 tsp smooth Dijon mustard

Pinch of sugar

Sea salt and pepper to taste

1 Tbsp finely chopped flat-leaf parsley

2 heads Boston or Bibb lettuce

2 cups gourmet fried root chips, slightly crushed

1. In a small bowl, whisk together the olive oil, lemon juice, garlic, mustard, sugar, salt, pepper and parsley. Taste it, make sure you love it, then set it aside.

2. Get out a big salad bowl. Tear apart the heads of lettuce, leaving the leaves mostly intact, and place in the bowl. Toss with dressing. Turn out onto a serving platter and sprinkle with root vegetable chips. Serve at once.

Dukkah-Dusted Carrot Fritters
with Herbed Yogurt

Vegetables meet a winning Egyptian spice blend (that you can also use on everything from chicken to pita schmeared with labneh) and an herby dip. When the family asks what's for dinner, just say, "Oh, you know, carrots," with your best Cleopatra wink. Then surprise them.

FOR THE HERBED YOGURT:

½ cup 2% plain yogurt

1 Tbsp finely chopped flat-leaf parsley

1 Tbsp finely chopped mint

Juice of ½ lemon

1 Tbsp olive oil

1 tsp honey

Sea salt and pepper to taste

FOR THE FRITTERS:

1 cup flour

½ tsp sea salt

¼ tsp pepper

1 tsp baking powder

1 cup dukkah, divided (recipe follows)

2 eggs

½ cup water

1 tsp olive oil

3 cups grated carrots (about 3 large)

Vegetable oil, for deep-frying

1. To make the herbed yogurt, in a small bowl, mix together the yogurt, parsley, mint, lemon juice, olive oil, honey, salt and pepper until smooth. Taste for seasoning, then cover and refrigerate for at least 30 minutes.

2. For the fritters, in a large bowl, combine the flour, salt, pepper, baking powder and ¼ cup dukkah. In another bowl, whisk the eggs, water and oil. Stir the egg mixture into the dry ingredients just until moistened. Fold in the carrots.

3. Heat 2-3 inches of oil in a large heavy-bottomed, high-sided skillet. It should reach 350°F or up to 365°F. Using two soup spoons to make oval-shaped little footballs (quenelles), drop the batter into the hot oil, making sure not to crowd the pan. Fry until golden brown, about 2 minutes on each side. Remove the fritters with a slotted spoon or tongs and transfer to a plate lined with paper towel to drain. You should wind up with about 12 fritters. Serve with the herbed yogurt and a small bowl of the remaining dukkah for more sprinkling.

Dukkah

MAKES ABOUT 1 CUP

½ cup salted roasted cashews (pistachios, almonds and hazelnuts are also nice), toasted and completely cooled

¼ cup coriander seeds

3 Tbsp sesame seeds

2 Tbsp cumin seeds

½ tsp dried mint

1 tsp kosher salt

¼ tsp pepper

1. Combine the nuts, coriander, sesame seeds, cumin, mint, salt and pepper in a food processor and pulse until it reaches a medium grind and is crumbly. You can also use a mortar and pestle. Transfer the nut mixture to a medium nonstick skillet and toast gently on medium-low heat, stirring constantly until just aromatic, about 3 minutes. Remove from the pan and set aside to cool. Store in an airtight container in the fridge for up to 1 month.

Spinach Bites with Honey Mustard

SERVES
8–10

I first ate these delicious, savory bites at my friend Joanna's house when her mom, Andrea, made them for a big party a couple of decades ago. I got the recipe from her and recently made them for a party of my own, and let's just say the ensuing years have not diminished their power. Full of spinach, buttery stuffing and Parmigiano-Reggiano, then dipped in honey mustard for added oomph, they go fast, so doubling the recipe isn't a bad idea.

2 (10 oz) packages frozen spinach, thawed

2 cups herbed stuffing mix (such as Pepperidge Farm or Stove Top), crushed

1 cup freshly grated Parmigiano-Reggiano

½ cup butter, melted

4 green onions, trimmed and finely chopped

3 eggs, beaten

Vegetable oil spray

Honey mustard, for serving

1. Preheat the oven to 350°F.

2. Place the thawed spinach in a clean tea towel and, using your hands and all of your strength, squeeze it until the spinach is as dry as you can get it.

3. In a large bowl, combine the spinach with the crushed stuffing, Parmigiano-Reggiano, butter, green onions and eggs. Mix well with your hands. Spray a baking sheet with vegetable oil, then form the spinach mixture into 1-inch balls. Place the balls on the baking sheet (spaced so they're not touching), and bake in the preheated oven for 10–15 minutes. These can be made ahead of time and warmed up in a 200°F oven before serving. They're also tasty at room temperature.

4. Pour the honey mustard into a pretty little dish and set it in the center of a large plate. Pile the spinach balls up and around the bowl and serve.

Pickled Beet Salad

Here, autumn turns into winter, and your suburban bagel brunch turns into a Swedish smorgasbord. This side salad is zingy, it's zany, it's full of fruits and vegetables, sour cream and mayonnaise. It shouldn't work, but it does.

FOR THE PICKLED BEETS:

8 medium beets

1 cup red wine vinegar

1 cup white vinegar

2 cups water

3 tsp kosher salt

1 cup sugar

FOR THE SALAD:

1 Tbsp smooth Dijon mustard

½ cup full-fat sour cream

4 Tbsp mayonnaise

¼ cup marinade from pickled beets

½ red onion, finely chopped

2 Granny Smith apples, cored and diced

2 stalks celery, thinly sliced

Sea salt and pepper to taste

1. To roast the beets, preheat the oven to 425°F. Wash and dry the beets, then wrap them tightly in foil and place on a baking sheet. Roast in the oven for 45 minutes, or until cooked through but not mushy. You can roast the beets ahead of time.

2. Combine both vinegars, the water, salt and sugar in a stainless-steel or other nonreactive saucepan. Give it a stir and bring to a boil for 1 minute, then turn off the heat and set aside.

3. Remove the peels from the beets. This is a messy job—I like to do it in the sink. Cut the peeled beets into 1-inch cubes. Put the prepared beets and the vinegar marinade in a glass dish, cover with a lid and refrigerate for at least 24 hours.

4. For the salad, mix together the mustard, sour cream, mayo and ¼ cup beet marinade. Drain the remaining marinade and toss the prepared beets with the creamy dressing, onions, apples and celery, then season with salt and pepper. Refrigerate until ready to serve.

French Onion Dip

Imagine if your favorite chip dip didn't come from a container or from a packet mixed into sour cream and mayo, but instead was made with care and deeply caramelized onions. Friends, this is that dip.

1 Tbsp butter

1 Tbsp olive oil

2 medium onions, finely sliced (about 2 cups)

½ tsp sugar

¾ tsp sea salt

½ cup 2% plain Greek yogurt

1 cup full-fat sour cream

½ cup mayonnaise

½ tsp garlic powder

Pepper to taste

Kettle chips, for dipping

Fresh vegetables, for dipping

1. In a large skillet over medium heat, combine the butter and oil. Add the onions, sugar and salt. Sauté for 10 minutes, stirring often, then reduce heat to low and continue cooking until the onions are deeply caramelized, about 15–20 minutes more. Remove from the heat and set aside to cool.

2. In a medium bowl, mix together the yogurt, sour cream, mayonnaise, garlic powder and pepper until smooth. Roughly chop the caramelized onions and stir into the dip. Refrigerate for at least 30 minutes, then stir again before serving with your favorite chips and fresh vegetables.

Crisp Cucumber & Radish Salad

Refreshingly crisp, crunchy and almost ethereal, this is a gentler take on a pickled salad, and the dill totally makes it. It's a pretty little dish that was made for sprucing up a sandwich plate.

3 large English cucumbers

1½ tsp sea salt

6 radishes, very thinly sliced

⅓ cup white vinegar

2 Tbsp cider vinegar

¼ cup plus 1 Tbsp sugar

2 Tbsp chopped dill

1. Peel the cucumbers and cut them in half lengthwise. Cut off the rough ends. Using a teaspoon or small melon baller, scoop out any seeds and watery center from each half, forming a shallow groove down the center. Then slice the cucumbers crosswise as thinly as possible.

2. Place the prepared cucumbers in a colander and sprinkle with the salt. Toss to combine and allow to stand for at least 1 hour or up to 2 hours. Do not rinse the salt off. Use your hands to gently squeeze handfuls of cucumbers to release any excess liquid. You can also use a tea towel to squeeze them dry.

3. In a nonreactive mixing bowl (basically, anything but aluminum), combine the white vinegar, cider vinegar and sugar, and stir until the sugar dissolves. Add the cucumbers, radishes and dill and stir to combine. Serve at room temperature, or refrigerate overnight and serve cold.

Spicy Sesame Cheese Straws

The spicy cheese straws from Harbord Bakery in Toronto were always on the menu at my best friend Natasha's house during her family's amazing parties. There were usually so many people packed into the Presses' house that I often had trouble staking out and then hoarding the delicate nibbles—so I learned to make this easy version myself.

1 egg

½ cup freshly grated Parmigiano-Reggiano

½ tsp red pepper flakes

½ package (1 sheet) frozen rolled puff pastry, thawed

1 Tbsp sesame seeds

1. Preheat the oven to 400°F and line a baking sheet with parchment paper.

2. In a small bowl, beat the egg well. Set aside. In another bowl, combine the Parmigiano-Reggiano and red pepper flakes. Set aside.

3. Brush the entire sheet of puff pastry with the egg wash, then slice in half lengthwise. Spread the cheese mixture over one half of the pastry, leaving a ¼-inch border on each edge. Then cover with the other half of the puff pastry, egg-wash side down. Gently press down to seal both halves together.

4. Slice the pastry into ½-inch strips widthwise. Holding one end of a strip, slowly twist the other side a few times and pinch the ends. Lay the twists on the prepared baking sheet as you go, placing them 1 inch apart, until all the twists are done. You should have 12. Brush each twist lightly with egg wash and sprinkle with sesame seeds. Bake in the preheated oven for 15–18 minutes, or until golden brown and cooked through.

Warm Marinated Olives

MAKES
ABOUT

4

CUPS

When you're pressed for time but want something ready to nibble on as soon as guests arrive, there's no greater go-to than a bowl of olives. With a little extra effort, you can make them your own by marinating them in a flavorful oil and then warming them up just before the party starts. It's the little things.

4 cups mixed olives, rinsed

1 clove garlic, thinly sliced

1 small lemon, cut into wedges then roughly chopped

2 tsp chopped rosemary

1 tsp red pepper flakes

Pepper to taste

¼ cup extra virgin olive oil

1. Toss the olives, garlic, lemon pieces, rosemary, red pepper flakes, pepper and olive oil together in a bowl and let sit at room temperature for a few hours. A few minutes before serving, warm the olive mixture in a pan over medium-low heat, then pour into a pretty decorative bowl, with a side bowl for the pits.

Instant Pickles

Did Jews invent pickles? Probably not. But as Italians and Spaniards put olives on the table with every meal, Ashkenazi Jews smack down a bowl of sour dills. Or at least they do in my house. I was so used to the cheek-sucking, lip-smacking sour dills of my youth that the first time I tried a sweet pickle I didn't understand what it was. It was almost like eating relish in solid form. These pickles are for those times when you're in the mood but someone left the cloudy jar in the fridge empty. They're crisper than you may be used to, but the taste is as refreshing as a picnic.

3 medium-size fresh pickling cucumbers

1 cup white vinegar

1½ tsp kosher salt

½ cup sugar

1 cup water

2 Tbsp chopped dill

1. Quarter the cucumbers lengthwise so you get four spears from each.

2. In a small saucepan, bring the vinegar, salt, sugar and water to a boil.

3. Place the prepared cucumbers in a bowl and pour the hot vinegar mixture overtop. Add the chopped dill. Let cool on the counter for 1 hour, then put in the fridge to chill. The pickles will keep for about 1 week, although they're so good, they probably won't last the day.

Passover Party Mix

Even during Passover, through all of the matzo suffering, you still want a little snickle-snackle to go along with your latest Netflix binge. Here I present all the great tastes of a cereal-based party snack, with none of the *chametz* (not kosher for Passover) guilt.

3 Tbsp butter

2 Tbsp Worcestershire sauce (see note)

1 tsp seasoned salt

½ tsp garlic powder

½ tsp onion powder

4 sheets egg matzo, broken into bite-size pieces

1 (8 oz) bag kettle-cooked potato chips

1 (1.75 oz) box soup nuts (*mandlen*)

1 cup mixed nuts

1. Preheat the oven to 250°F.

2. Melt the butter in a small bowl in the microwave, then stir in the Worcestershire sauce, seasoned salt, garlic powder and onion powder. Place the matzo, chips, soup nuts and mixed nuts in a large roasting pan and toss with the seasoned butter until well coated.

3. Bake for 1 hour in the preheated oven, stirring every 15 minutes or so. When toasty and smelling like snack-food heaven, remove and cool. Best when eaten fresh.

Note: If you're strictly kosher for Passover, substitute the Worcestershire with a kosher for Passover soy sauce.

Chapter 4

EAT! EAT!

(Pareve, Dairy & Meat)

A Cuisine to Call Our Own

A middle-aged businessman sits alone in a maroon booth at a linen-swathed table in an upscale Chinese restaurant. A plate mounded with glistening morsels of chicken is placed before him. As he literally rubs his palms in anticipation, he asks his mandarin-jacketed waiter for chopsticks, and then, upon his return, a knife. "I love this sauce!" he exclaims, almost to himself, but loud enough that, seated nearby, we can measure his enthusiasm. "It's not sickly sweet like the General Tso's everywhere else." The waiter nods the nod of a man who has been through this before.

The cloth napkin the businessman has tucked like a bib over his crisp pink dress shirt only adds to the picture of his boyish enthusiasm for the food. It is as if every bite of chopstick-held chicken is a trip back to the high-school bleachers when he finally got to third base with his first sweetheart. "They basically invented Szechuan in this city, you know?!" he half-shouts over to me—this city being Montreal, where I am sitting at L'Orchidée de Chine on Peel Street awaiting my own meal, a meal I know is unique to this place.

In the 1960s, Ruby Foo's opened on Decarie Boulevard. The pulsing neon sign promising Chinese *and* Western dishes helped usher in an era of high-end Chinese food, where the restaurant's maître d' would serve Pierre Elliott Trudeau *canard à l'orange* tableside. Likeminded spots followed, including Piment Rouge, Le Chrysanthème, Zen and a handful of others. The upscale food and service was the perfect pairing for Montreal's old-school business elite (read: Jewish *schmata* business owners). It was an acceptable interpretation of the Chinese food they had grown up on and craved. Historically, Jews and Chinese people had lived in close proximity in the denser North American urban centers (frequently due to the timing of their immigration waves), whether it be Manhattan's Lower East Side or Toronto's Kensington Market. And unlike many other ethnic immigrants at the turn of the last century, Chinese restaurateurs, for the most part, weren't anti-Semitic, so their restaurants gave Jews a sense of security. And exoticism. What's more, Chinese cuisine didn't mix milk with meat (adding a faux kosher appeal). That the restaurants remained open on Christmas cemented this special cross-cultural relationship.

All of these details played a role in Montreal's Jewish dining crowd liking their Chinese through the '60s and '70s. But then in the '80s, a new style of highbrow Chinese

arrived in Montreal. It riffed on the dishes Montrealers yearned for, but was sweeter, crisper and made from a higher quality of ingredients, all dressed up in a bow tie and a toque for a thriving local audience. With glamorous decor, white-gloved waiters, French wines and exquisite (if not wholly authentic) Far East classics, it paired neatly with the changing nature of a clientele who were part of a rapidly changing Canada. The food was tailor-made for a country waking up to the diversity of the world. Oh yeah, and it was delicious.

This is what the guests at L'Orchidée de Chine have come for on the day I am there. It's cold out, but the sharp blue Montreal winter sky warms the room through the windows, as elegantly coiffed women hand over furs for careful hanging. The restaurant is set in two stories, with a curvaceous staircase winding up from the sun-drenched entrance. Many customers are seated on the main floor by the windows, while upstairs in an almost morosely dark room, you can hear soft mid-tempo jazz. By 12:30 p.m., every table, vinyl banquette and vaguely Chinese red-upholstered high-back is occupied by suave, graying business types wearing designer glasses. Brother and sister co-owners George and Eva Lau greet them all like old friends.

"The restaurant has been here since 1984," Eva Lau tells me when she sits down at my banquette. "The idea was, we'd seen too many Americanized Chinese restaurants serving Cantonese. We thought that needed to change because it had always just been Cantonese Chinese in North America." They decided to bring in a different cuisine from mid-20th-century Canadian Chinese food; that is, the stuff that diners were already accustomed to—blistered-fat eggrolls, deep-fried chicken balls in neon orange sauce, and chop suey (the original cultural mash-up). The cuisine the Laus had in mind had the fiery, bold notes of Szechuan. "But of course not authentic Szechuan, because we had to make it a little different for the local tastes," she explains. The idea was to offer an alternative to the family-run "Chinese and Western" institutions dotting Canada's railway towns.

The regulars at L'Orchidée de Chine may not be Chinese, but this is most definitely their food, created to suit the tastes of the new Canada that was emerging in the late Trudeau years, when multiculturalism and broader immigration were welcoming assorted cultures (and their cuisines). Trudeau's vision of the country encouraged newcomers to stay true to their roots instead of blending into an American-style melting pot. Thinking about all this while talking to Eva Lau makes me wonder about the nature of authenticity and whether *authentic* necessarily means *better*. If we bastardize another's dishes, is it an homage, or simply smart business? Montrealers in the mid-'80s, after all, were embracing the cultures of the world, but they were still shaping them to suit their tastes. Tradition is important, but not so much if old Saul fries his tongue on Szechuan peppercorns.

Reading all this deftly, the Laus set out to embrace the inauthentic, instructing their chefs to make their Szechuan Montreal-friendly (a hint sweeter and a touch less spicy), while at the same time creating a dining experience that had a look and feel that suited their heady 1980s roster of regulars, including local politicians and visiting stars like Marlon Brando, Anthony Hopkins and Nicole Kidman. A tradition that continues: Hugh Jackman recently popped by for takeout. Their target market is not-necessarily-Chinese Montrealers, so instead of fish being presented with the head and tail intact—a sign of freshness in China—and the tastier dark meat being spun into chicken dishes, the Laus serve fish in fillets and use only white breast meat. Shrimp are never served in their shells. Lost in translation from Szechuan to Montreal are the juiciness of dark meat and the licking of fingers after peeling shrimp shells, but this is not bastardization, just adaptation.

"And we decided to do French service," Lau tells me, highlighting another touch they thought Montrealers would warm to. This means waiters divide dishes from the serving plate for the customer instead of putting the dishes in the middle of the table for diners to serve themselves family style. Napkins are expertly folded into exotic fans. There are votive candles on the tables, a perfect clipped fresh orchid lazily floating in each. "We wanted to give a proper service, introduce a new idea of Chinese dining in Montreal." On the menu it's not even called Szechuan. It's "Setzchwan." Three layers removed from the original spelling, and an overt declaration that this is Szechuan

westernized just so, created with purpose, but without malice.

My lunch guest, my pal Sarah Musgrave, joins me and we place our order. Lau recommends their most popular dishes, including the silky pork-stuffed dumplings bathed in a mildly piquant peanut sauce, mini ribs that end up tasting just like porky garlic caramel, black pepper chicken tossed with flash-fried spinach, and crunchy orange beef. Musgrave, a former restaurant critic, figures the place is all about nostalgia. In China, she says, Szechuan is the most popular cuisine. It's known for its variety of spices and notes that hit on flowery, bitter, sour, sweet and smoky. It's a cuisine with depth and complexity, though in North America it's been unfairly pigeonholed as a chili and pepper gun show. Kung Pao chicken and mapo tofu are two of the more famous dishes. "This is all really just a reimagining of what Montreal would want from Szechuan food," says Musgrave through a mouthful.

Indeed, the incredibly tasty plate of *Setzchwan* in front of me might be the most authentically inauthentic food I've ever tasted, but that does not make it a lesser-than hybrid. Rather, I see it as a local interpretation of a foreign cuisine, something altered, in the same way some theater companies might mount *Hamlet* set in modern times to make it easier for us to see through to the play's human depths. The food on our plate isn't Szechuan. It is a Montreal portal delivering us to the idea of Szechuan.

I had been to China a few months earlier, and there is no doubt—this is not that. In Quanzhou, in Fujian province, a lunch buffet can be a mind-bending journey into oil-baked clams, braised river eel and sandworm jelly. Woe is the tourist who thinks she's pushing the cappuccino button on the coffee machine. Out dribbles purple sweet taro juice instead. Taking the bullet train farther into the mountains, from Fuzhou to Wuyishanbei, I ate at an al fresco restaurant situated over a river with a working bamboo waterwheel, the table strewn with five-spice chicken, cucumber with jellyfish, spicy snails, whole smoked duck and tofu so fresh it was still draining through the cheesecloth

into its wooden box. Every bite had a sense of place. From village to town to city, I did not eat the same dish twice in China, which raises the question: How do you define "authentic" Szechuan in Canada when the palate moves a thousand different directions even in Szechuan, China? Is authenticity just a state of mind? Why would or should I expect to find Wuyishanbei jellyfish in downtown Montreal, and would I even want to eat it if I wasn't sitting beside a bamboo waterwheel on a dewy afternoon?

A few years ago, I participated in a matzo ball competition at a local deli in Toronto. I make delicious matzo balls—this is a fact not open to interpretation. David Sax, the noted culture writer and author of *Save the Deli* and *The Tastemakers*, was a judge at the blind tasting. Sax approached me immediately following my loss, and without officially knowing which balls were mine, he'd nevertheless pegged my herb-flecked losers. "Fresh dill in the matzo balls, Rosen? You know you can't do that."

But I wondered then and wonder now, who gets to define the definitive version of a dish? Were my matzo balls not fluffy and flavorful? Or were they the Kung Pao chicken interlopers of the *kneidlach* world? The rest of the matzo balls were a variation on the same prosaic yet authentic theme, and one of them was deemed the winner. Which helps explain why Ashkenazi food has three basic dishes in its repertoire (matzo ball soup, brisket and kugel, in case you were wondering). Some things are apparently meant to stay the same. Forever. Does that

make them authentic? Or fossilized? I recently followed up with Sax on some of these questions. "I was wrong about the matzo balls," he courageously admitted. "They should not follow any script."

The Laus at L'Orchidée de Chine were serving elevated Chinese food when no one else was, at a time when Canada was opening itself up to the world. Of course, being Canadian, we still had to moderate things somewhat. In any case, not only is it impossible to fully transport the authentic (as bits of it inevitably evaporate in the vapor trails over the Pacific), it's also not fully desirable. If something is changing, that means it's alive. The same goes for Jewish cuisine. That's why I add fresh herbs to my matzo balls (even if Sax doesn't like them) and fresh pineapple to my sweet-and-sour meatballs. It's also why I cook with quinoa. It may not be authentic, but it's delicious. And that's the beauty of L'Orchidée de Chine, where you go because you *don't* want authentic Szechuan. You go because you want not-too-spicy orange beef and sweeter-and-milder-than-anything-you'd-ever-find-in-China General Tso's chicken. You want authentic *Setzchwan*. Because when it comes to General Tso's with white breast meat, its inauthenticity is what makes it worth having.

That, and the sauce.

Roasted Salmon with Horseradish Sauce & Pickled Onions

A head-turning dish full of vibrant flavors, from pickled onions to herbs to horseradish, and colors to match (hello, pink and fuchsia), this side of salmon could easily usurp gefilte fish at your next Seder.

FOR THE PICKLED ONIONS:

½ cup red wine vinegar

1 tsp kosher salt

¼ cup sugar

½ cup water

½ red onion, thinly sliced

FOR THE SALMON:

3½ lb whole side skin-on salmon

1 Tbsp olive oil

1 Tbsp Herbes de Provence

½ tsp sea salt

Pepper to taste

FOR THE HORSERADISH SAUCE:

½ cup mayonnaise

3 Tbsp jarred beet horseradish

Juice of ½ lemon

1. To make the pickled onions, place the vinegar, salt, sugar and water in a small saucepan and bring to a boil. Place the prepared onions in a bowl and pour the hot vinegar mixture overtop. Let cool on the counter for 1 hour, then put in the fridge to chill.

2. For the horseradish sauce, stir together the mayonnaise, beet horseradish and lemon juice. Cover and refrigerate.

3. Preheat the oven to 450°F.

4. Line a large rimmed baking sheet with foil or parchment paper. Place the salmon, skin side down, on the baking sheet. Rub with olive oil and sprinkle with Herbes de Provence, salt and pepper. Roast the salmon in the preheated oven until just opaque in the center, about 20 minutes. Serve with pickled onions and horseradish sauce on the side.

Lamb Stew with Pea Dumplings

This is my signature recipe. It's the one my family asks for the most, and the one that never results in any leftovers. If lamb isn't your thing, it works just as well with stewing beef. Plunked down in the middle of the table in a big pot, there's no better meal on a cold winter night.

FOR THE STEW:

3 lb boneless lamb shoulder, cut into 2-inch cubes

2 Tbsp flour

Sea salt and pepper to taste

¼ tsp cayenne pepper

2 Tbsp olive oil

2 large onions, chopped

2 Tbsp tomato paste

1 Tbsp honey

½ cup water

2 cups dry red wine

3 large carrots, cut into 1-inch pieces

FOR THE DUMPLINGS:

1½ cups flour

2 tsp baking powder

½ tsp sea salt

Pepper to taste

½ tsp dried rosemary, finely chopped

3 Tbsp vegetable shortening

About ¾ cup water

½ cup frozen peas, thawed

1. To make the stew, trim any fat or gristle off the lamb cubes. In a large bowl, mix the flour with the salt, pepper and cayenne. Add the lamb, toss to coat and pat off any excess with paper towel.

2. In a large pot, heat the olive oil over high heat, then add the cubes of meat, turning them every so often so they are well browned. Make sure not to crowd the pot. You'll likely have to sear the cubes in a couple of batches.

3. Once all the meat is browned, return it all to the pot, reduce the heat to medium and add the chopped onions. Let the onions sweat with the meat for several minutes. Add the tomato paste and honey, then stir in ½ cup water, scraping off any browned bits from the bottom of the pan. Cook for 5 minutes, then add the wine, stir and bring to a boil. Taste for seasoning, adding more salt and pepper if needed. Reduce the heat

to a low simmer, cover the pot and let the stew cook for 2 hours, stirring about every 20 minutes.

4. After 2 hours, toss in the carrots and cook for 10 minutes. If the stew gets a little dry at any point, add a bit more water.

5. Meanwhile, make the dumplings. In a bowl, mix together the flour, baking powder, salt, pepper and rosemary. Add the shortening, mixing it in with a fork so it breaks down and the mixture looks grainy. Slowly add the water until the dough is light but solid and can be easily dropped from a soup spoon. Stir the peas into the dough.

6. Remove the pot lid and stir. Wet a soup spoon, scoop up mounds of dumpling dough and drop them into the stew. Space the dumplings out around the perimeter of the pot first, then work your way in. Do not stir! Cover the pot and allow the dumplings to cook for 20 minutes. Serve immediately.

Quinoa-Tofu Bowl with Greens & Green Goddess

This is an example of how Jews eat today. And probably how they ate in the hippy-dippy 1970s. We'll eat healthfully, just as long as it tastes good. I'm here to tell you that with quinoa, tofu, hearty greens, broccoli and peas, all topped with a glorious green goddess dressing and salty cashews, this tastes great.

FOR THE GREEN GODDESS DRESSING:

1 cup mayonnaise

1 cup sour cream

1 bunch tarragon, leaves removed from stems

1 bunch chives, roughly chopped

1 clove garlic, chopped

1 tsp anchovy paste

Juice of 1 lemon

Sea salt and pepper to taste

2 cups water

1 cup quinoa, rinsed

1 (14 oz) package extra-firm tofu

Sea salt and pepper to taste

2 Tbsp cornstarch

1 Tbsp vegetable oil

1 small bunch broccoli, trimmed and cut into florets (about 2 cups)

1 bunch rapini, stems trimmed, cut into thirds (about 3 cups)

1 cup frozen peas, thawed and rinsed

2 cups baby kale

½ cup salted roasted cashews

1. Make the dressing by placing the mayonnaise, sour cream, tarragon, chives, garlic, anchovy paste and lemon juice in a blender and blending until smooth. Add salt and pepper to taste. This makes 2 cups—you won't need it all, but leftovers store well in the fridge for several days.

2. Place the 2 cups water in a medium saucepan, add salt and bring to a boil. Add the quinoa, stir, cover, reduce heat and simmer until quinoa is tender, about 12 minutes. Remove from the heat and let stand for 15 minutes, then fluff the quinoa with a fork. Set aside.

3. Remove the tofu from its package and pat dry. Cut into 1-inch cubes and season liberally with salt and pepper, then toss to coat in cornstarch. Heat the vegetable oil

in a large nonstick skillet over medium heat. Add the tofu cubes and fry until lightly golden and crispy, about 6–8 minutes, turning now and then.

4. Using the rinsed-out quinoa pot, bring 2 inches of water to a simmer. Add the prepared broccoli and rapini and steam for 4 minutes. Drain and rinse with cold water in a colander. Pat off excess water.

5. To assemble, heap the quinoa into a large serving bowl and top with a mélange of the steamed green vegetables, cold peas and cubes of crispy tofu. Drizzle with a healthy dose of the green goddess dressing and garnish with fresh baby kale and cashews.

Fried Chicken & Slaw

SERVES

8–10

When I was growing up, KFC (née Kentucky Fried Chicken) was a monthly treat in our house, eaten out of paper boxes after swim class. My brothers loved it, but there was something about the secret spicing that turned me off, so I never ate the stuff. Yet I loved the coleslaw almost more than ice cream, and that's the style of slaw I've created here to go along with my delicious fried chicken seasoned with four non-secret ingredients and a whisper of matzo meal. Please note: If you're kosher, do not eat the slaw and the chicken together.

FOR THE SLAW:

1 small head green cabbage

1 medium carrot, peeled

½ cup mayonnaise

⅓ cup sugar

¼ cup milk

¼ cup buttermilk

Juice of 1 lemon

1 Tbsp white vinegar

½ tsp sea salt

Pepper to taste

2 Tbsp finely chopped sweet onion

FOR THE FRIED CHICKEN:

2 cups flour

½ cup matzo meal

2 tsp sea salt, divided

1 tsp pepper, divided

1 tsp garlic powder, divided

1 tsp cayenne pepper, divided

2 (3 lb) frying chickens, cut up (or use your favorite chicken parts)

1 cup vegetable shortening

1. To make the slaw, finely chop the cabbage and carrot in a food processor. In a large bowl, combine the mayonnaise, sugar, milk, buttermilk, lemon juice, vinegar, salt and pepper. Whisk until smooth. Add the cabbage, carrots and onion and stir well to combine. Refrigerate for at least 3 hours before serving.

2. For the chicken, combine the flour, matzo meal and 1 teaspoon salt, ½ teaspoon pepper, ½ teaspoon garlic powder and ½ teaspoon cayenne in a large plastic or paper bag. Line a baking sheet with parchment paper. Season the chicken with the remaining pepper, garlic powder and cayenne, then add a few pieces of chicken at a time to the flour bag. Shake to coat, then transfer the chicken to the baking sheet and let sit for 15 minutes.

3. In a large cast-iron skillet, heat the shortening to 365°F (medium-high heat). Shallow-fry the chicken for 25–35 minutes without lowering the heat, turning once or twice for even browning. You will have to do this in several batches so as not to overcrowd the pan. The chicken is done when the internal temperature reaches 165°F. Drain the chicken on a plate lined with paper towel. Sprinkle with the remaining 1 teaspoon of salt, as needed. Serve hot and crispy.

Sweet & Sour Meatballs

One of the dishes we ate most in our house when I was growing up was Swedish meatballs. I think my mom got the recipe off the label of either Welch's grape jelly or Heinz chili sauce, because, besides ground beef, those were the two ingredients in which she'd simmer the balls. She still makes them and we still eat them happily today. This is my take on sweet-and-sour meatballs. A lot fresher, albeit with a ketchup tip of the hat to the 1980s.

4 lb lean ground beef

3 eggs

½ cup plain breadcrumbs

2 tsp sea salt, plus extra to taste

1 tsp pepper, plus extra to taste

6 medium tomatoes, roughly chopped

2 onions, roughly chopped

2 medium carrots, roughly chopped

1 pineapple, peeled, cored and roughly chopped

3 Tbsp olive oil

1 tsp ground ginger

2 Tbsp honey

6 Tbsp ketchup

3 Tbsp red wine vinegar

Mashed potatoes or rice, for serving

1. In a large bowl, combine the beef, eggs, breadcrumbs, salt and pepper. Mix well, then roll into 1-inch bite-size meatballs.

2. Place the prepped tomatoes, onions and carrots in a food processor and chop until smooth, then add the pineapple and pulse so that it's still a bit chunky.

3. Transfer the mixture to a very large pot and add the oil, ginger, honey, ketchup and vinegar, plus salt and pepper to taste, then bring to a boil. Lower heat to a simmer, add meatballs and cook, partially covered, for 2 hours. Serve with mashed potatoes or rice.

Note: Depending on the sweetness of your vegetables and pineapple, you may want to adjust with more ketchup, vinegar, salt, etc. before serving, in order to hit that perfect balance. Taste your food!

Miami Ribs

When I came up with the idea for this cookbook, the first thing most people asked me was whether I was going to include recipes for brisket and for Miami ribs. With their extreme savory, sticky, sweet meatiness, both are favorites of Jews and non-Jews alike. I'm happy to say that the answer is a resounding yes (see p. 188 for my brisket).

2 Tbsp vegetable oil

3 lb beef brisket short ribs (aka Miami ribs)

½ cup dark soy sauce

½ cup packed brown sugar

1 tsp dry mustard

1 Tbsp Worcestershire sauce

3 cloves garlic, finely chopped

½ cup water

2 green onions, trimmed and thinly sliced, for garnish

1. Preheat the oven to 350°F.

2. Heat the oil in a large skillet over medium heat. Brown the ribs in the hot oil, a few strips at a time.

3. Meanwhile, in a large ovenproof baking dish, combine the soy sauce, brown sugar, dry mustard, Worcestershire, garlic and water. Whisk well.

4. Add the seared ribs to the marinade and toss to coat. Cover tightly with foil and bake in the preheated oven for 2 hours. Remove the foil and cook for another 30 minutes. Sprinkle with green onions and serve immediately.

Chicken Schnitzel

4

From what I can recall, the first time I went to Israel for my older brother Marty's bar mitzvah, we ate only two dishes during the two-week trip: falafel and schnitzel. The culinary scene in Israel has exploded since then, but let me tell you, schnitzel is still one of the most simply satisfying meals you can eat.

4 boneless, skinless chicken breast halves (about 6 oz each), tenders removed

2 tsp sea salt

Pepper to taste

1 cup flour

2 eggs, well beaten

2 cups panko breadcrumbs

1 cup vegetable oil

1 lemon, cut into wedges

1. Place one piece of chicken in a resealable plastic bag and pound it with a meat tenderizer or a rolling pin until about ¼ inch thick and even all around. Repeat with the remaining three pieces of meat. Season all over with salt and pepper and set aside.

2. Place the flour on a dinner plate, the beaten eggs on another and the panko crumbs on a third.

3. In a large cast-iron skillet over medium heat, heat the oil to 375°F. Line a baking sheet with paper towel for draining.

4. Dip a chicken cutlet in flour and shake off any excess. Dip in the egg, letting any excess drain off, then press into the panko crumbs until well coated and transfer to a plate. Repeat with the remaining cutlets.

5. When the oil is hot, fry the schnitzel, a piece at a time, for about 2 minutes on each side, or until golden brown and cooked though. Drain on the paper towel and repeat with the other three pieces. Sprinkle with salt while still hot.

6. Serve with a wedge of lemon and a green salad or boiled potatoes sprinkled with parsley.

Four-Ingredient Weeknight Chicken

Sometimes you've just got to get dinner on the table without much planning and fussing, using what you've got in the fridge. That's where this chicken recipe comes in handy. It also happens to be super-delicious. Throw some baby potatoes into the bottom of the pan first and you've got a schmaltzy side, baked right into the main dish.

8 bone-in, skin-on chicken thighs

Kosher salt and pepper to taste

1 medium red onion, peeled and cut into thin wedges

20 large green olives

2 medium seedless navel oranges (or 1 large)

1. Preheat the oven to 375°F.

2. In a large baking dish or roasting pan, place the chicken thighs in a single layer, skin side up. Season with salt and pepper. Spread the onion wedges and olives around the baking dish.

3. If using medium oranges, juice and zest 1 orange, then slice the second orange into thin half-moon slices. If using 1 large orange, juice and zest half and slice the other half. Spread the orange slices around the baking dish, then pour the juice all over the chicken.

4. Bake, uncovered, for 50 minutes to 1 hour, or until the chicken is cooked through and browned. Remove from the oven and let sit for 5-10 minutes before serving with bread, rice or roasted baby potatoes.

The Burger

If you've ever been to California, or have followed stars on Instagram during their post-Oscars burger runs, you'll know about In-N-Out Burger. Its "not-so-secret menu" includes the Animal Style burger, comprising mustard fried onto a beef patty, a toasted bun, pickles, a slice of tomato, leaf lettuce, a Thousand Island–style sauce, grilled onions and cheese. I've ditched the cheese in my version, so it's all kosher.

FOR THE CARAMELIZED ONIONS:

1 Tbsp vegetable oil

1 medium onion, finely chopped (about 1½ cups)

Good pinch of sea salt

FOR THE SPECIAL SAUCE:

4 Tbsp mayonnaise

2 Tbsp ketchup

1 Tbsp sweet relish

½ tsp sugar

½ tsp white vinegar

FOR THE BURGERS:

4 soft hamburger buns

1 lb lean ground beef

Sea salt and pepper to taste

½ Tbsp vegetable oil

4 tsp yellow mustard

1 dill pickle, thinly sliced into rounds

4 slices tomato

4 whole leaves iceberg lettuce

Ketchup (optional)

1. Heat 1 tablespoon vegetable oil in a large nonstick skillet over medium-low heat. Brown the onions along with a good pinch of salt. Sauté for about 25 minutes, or until meltingly tender and golden brown. Stir often. If the pan goes a bit dry, add 1 teaspoon water at a time, not extra oil. When the onions are cooked, set aside.

2. To make the special sauce, combine the mayonnaise, ketchup, relish, sugar and vinegar in a small bowl. Set aside.

3. Open the hamburger buns and toast, cut sides down, in a large nonstick skillet, until brown and toasty, about 1 minute. Set aside.

(continued)

4. Form the ground beef into four evenly-sized patties. Season each side generously with salt and pepper. Using the cleaned bun pan, heat the ½ tablespoon oil over medium-high. Add the burger patties and cook, without moving them, until well browned and crusty on the first side, about 3 minutes. While they're cooking, spread 1 teaspoon mustard on the raw side of each patty with a spoon. Flip the patties with a spatula so the mustard side is down, and continue cooking for 1–2 minutes.

5. Layer each bottom bun with about 1 tablespoon special sauce, a few pickle slices and a slice of tomato. Place the cooked patties on top, and finish each one with caramelized onions. Top with crisp lettuce, a bit of ketchup if you please, and the lid of the toasted bun. Serve at once.

Spicy Jewish-Chinese Chicken Wings

They're Jewish because you say "oy vey" while eating them, they're that spicy. Meanwhile, the surprising five-spice undertone and cilantro and green onion overtones make them implausibly addictive. Also, they're baked, not fried, so mazel tov.

2 lb tipped chicken wings

¼ cup cornstarch

2 Tbsp vegetable oil

1 Tbsp sea salt

1 tsp Chinese five-spice powder

1 tsp cayenne pepper

3 green onions, trimmed and thinly sliced, for garnish

2 jalapeños, thinly sliced, for garnish

1 big handful cilantro leaves, for garnish

1 lime, quartered, for garnish

1. Preheat the oven to 425°F.

2. Cut the wings in half at the joint and place in a large bowl along with the cornstarch. Toss to coat, then transfer the wings to a plate, dusting off excess cornstarch. Dispose of any remaining cornstarch, then return the wings to the same cleaned bowl. Drizzle with oil and toss with salt, five-spice powder and cayenne to coat.

3. Line a baking sheet with parchment paper (you may need two baking sheets so as not to crowd the wings) and evenly spread out the wings. Bake for 30 minutes, or until cooked through and crisp. Transfer to a platter and sprinkle with green onions, jalapeños, cilantro and a squirt of lime juice.

Flank Steak with Gremolata

Steak doesn't always mean expensive. I love nothing better than a nice flank steak: it's lean, it's affordable and it serves a crowd. It's almost like the barbecued version of a brisket. Flank steak is best when simply seasoned and seared on the stovetop or barbecue for just a few minutes on each side, then rested and thinly sliced against the grain. While your steak is resting for 10 minutes, perk it up by preparing gremolata, a loose, citrus-hit, herbaceous topping that brings out the summer in steak.

FOR THE STEAK:	FOR THE GREMOLATA:	FOR THE ARUGULA SALAD:
1 tsp olive oil	½ cup flat-leaf parsley	5 oz baby arugula
1½ lb flank steak, room temperature	Zest of 1 lemon	1 green onion, trimmed and thinly sliced
Kosher salt and pepper to taste	1 tsp orange zest	Juice of 1 lemon
2 cups cherry or grape tomatoes	½ tsp kosher salt	1 Tbsp olive oil
½ red onion, sliced into rings	2 cloves garlic	Sea salt and pepper to taste
Pinch of red pepper flakes	2 Tbsp extra virgin olive oil	

1. To prepare the steak, heat the olive oil in a large pan over medium-high heat. Generously season both sides of the steak with salt and pepper, and add to the hot pan. Sear on the first side for 3–4 minutes, then likewise on the second side. Remove from the pan and set aside, but keep the pan on the heat and add the tomatoes, onion rings and red pepper flakes. Sauté the vegetables in the steak drippings, stirring often, for 2–3 minutes, or until the onions soften and the tomatoes start to burst. Remove from the heat and set aside to rest.

2. To make the gremolata, finely chop the parsley, lemon zest, orange zest, salt and garlic, and mix to combine. Transfer to a small bowl and stir in the olive oil.

3. In a large bowl, toss the arugula with the green onion, lemon juice, olive oil and salt and pepper to taste.

4. When the steak has rested for at least 10 minutes, thinly slice it against the grain. Place on a platter, surrounded by arugula salad, tomatoes and onions and topped with the gremolata. Serve at once, or chill for lunch the next day.

Roasted Garlic & Three-Cheese Skillet Pizza

This recipe is more about the method than necessarily making this pizza with these toppings. Once I discovered the joy and ease of making pizza in a skillet, I never looked back to my sheet pans or pizza stone. (Just kidding, I don't own a pizza stone.) Crisp on the bottom, fluffy in the center and properly caramelized on top, you'll love this garlic and cheese combo, but feel free to make a simple margarita or go to town with your favorite toppings.

1 head garlic

2 tsp olive oil

½ lb ball raw pizza dough, room temperature (see note)

1 tsp sesame seeds

1 cup shredded mozzarella

½ cup crumbled goat's cheese

¼ cup grated Parmigiano-Reggiano

½ tsp Herbes de Provence

1 red chili, thinly sliced

1 Tbsp honey

1. Preheat the oven to 350°F.

2. To roast the garlic, lop about ½ inch off the top of the whole head. Place the remaining garlic on a piece of foil, drizzle with a touch of olive oil, wrap the foil tightly around the garlic, then roast for 40–50 minutes, or until soft. Allow to cool slightly, then squeeze the roasted garlic into a bowl. Set aside.

3. Raise the oven temperature to 450°F.

4. Oil an 8-inch cast-iron skillet. On a lightly floured surface, roll the pizza dough out to about a 9-inch round and transfer to the skillet. Flip the dough over in the skillet so that both sides are oiled. Sprinkle with sesame seeds, especially around the edges, and gently press the dough evenly in the skillet so that it rises slightly up the sides of the pan. Bake in the preheated oven for 5 minutes.

5. Remove the par-baked pizza shell from the oven and spread with roasted garlic. Sprinkle evenly with the three cheeses, then the Herbes de Provence and the chili.

6. Bake for 15 minutes more, or until the pizza is cooked through and the cheese is melted and slightly browned. Drizzle with honey. Run a knife around the edges of the skillet to be sure it's not sticking. Slice and serve at once.

Note: You can find raw pizza dough balls in the bakery section of most supermarkets. They usually come as 1 lb balls, so you'll need to halve one for this recipe.

General Tso's Chicken

4–6

Everyone's favorite Chinese chicken dish comes home to roost. A large, weathered wok comes in handy here, but any big, deep skillet will do. Pair the saucy fried chicken with rice and stir-fried greens for homemade delivery done right. It may not be authentic, but authentic isn't what we're after here.

FOR THE SAUCE:

4 Tbsp dark soy sauce

2 Tbsp tomato paste

2 Tbsp seasoned rice vinegar

4 Tbsp Chinese rice wine or dry sherry

4 Tbsp brown sugar

½ cup water or chicken broth

1 Tbsp cornstarch mixed with 1 Tbsp cold water

FOR THE CHICKEN:

2 Tbsp dark soy sauce

2 eggs, lightly beaten

½ tsp pepper

4 Tbsp cornstarch

2 lb boneless, skinless chicken breasts, patted dry and cut into bite-size pieces

3 cups vegetable oil for deep-frying, plus 2 Tbsp for stir-frying

About 10 small dried red chilies

6 cloves garlic, sliced

2 Tbsp finely chopped fresh ginger

2 tsp sesame oil

4 green onions, trimmed and thinly sliced

Steamed rice, for serving

1. To make the sauce, combine the soy sauce, tomato paste, seasoned rice vinegar, rice wine, brown sugar, water and cornstarch in a bowl, whisking to dissolve the tomato paste and sugar. Set aside.

2. For the chicken, in a large bowl, combine the soy sauce, eggs, pepper and cornstarch. Add the chicken and evenly coat.

3. Heat 3 cups oil in a wok to around 370°F and line a large plate with paper towel. Carefully add the chicken to the hot oil, a few pieces at a time, and deep-fry until crispy, about 3–4 minutes. Remove and drain on the paper towel.

(continued)

4. When all the chicken is fried, drain the wok of oil and wipe clean. (Note: Do not pour oil down the drain. To properly dispose, pour it into a resealable jar and throw it in the trash.) Heat the remaining 2 tablespoons oil and, when hot, add the dried chilies, garlic and ginger. Stir-fry until aromatic, about 30 seconds, then add the sauce and stir until it thickens, 1–2 minutes.

5. Return the deep-fried chicken to the wok and toss to coat with the sauce for 2 minutes. Drizzle with sesame oil and garnish with green onions. Serve at once with a side of steamed rice.

Boobie Ronnie's Fricassee

On my dad's side of the family, two brothers married two sisters, so the families were tight and the genes were even tighter. My Boobie Ronnie and her sisters, Molly and Sue, all made a variation of a "poor man's" stew called fricassee, which used the offcuts of chicken, veal and beef. That's the beauty of family and tradition: when you share the same recipes, it's as if you're all gathered around one giant Shabbat table.

FOR THE MEATBALLS:

1½ lb ground veal (or beef or chicken)

1 egg, beaten

¼ cup plain breadcrumbs

½ tsp garlic powder

Sea salt and pepper to taste

4 Tbsp olive oil

2 sweet onions, diced

3 stalks celery, chopped

2 cups sliced cremini mushrooms

3 cups chicken stock

2 cups water

1 cup tomato sauce

1 lb chicken wings, cut into halves

4 boneless, skinless chicken thighs, cut into bite-size pieces

Pepper to taste

3 Tbsp flour

1 tsp garlic powder

3 Tbsp sweet paprika

Juice of 1 lemon

¼ cup brown sugar

Sea salt to taste

¼ cup chopped flat-leaf parsley, for garnish

1. To prepare the meatballs, combine the ground veal with the egg, breadcrumbs, garlic powder, salt and pepper in a medium bowl. Form into ½-inch balls and set aside.

2. Heat the oil in a large pot over medium heat, and cook the onions, celery and mushrooms until softened, about 8–10 minutes. Add the chicken stock, water and tomato sauce to the pot. Bring to a boil, then lower heat to a simmer.

3. In a large bowl, combine the chicken wings and thighs, black pepper, flour, garlic powder and paprika. Toss the chicken in the spice mixture, then transfer to the pot. Stir in the lemon juice, brown sugar, salt and additional pepper to taste. Gently add the meatballs to the pot. Partially cover and simmer for 1½ hours. Chill overnight. Skim the fat that rises to the top, reheat on the stove or in the oven, adjust seasoning, garnish with parsley and serve as an appetizer with challah. It's tradition.

Chopped Liver & Salami Sandwiches

Bring the deli to your kitchen with this heart-stopping old-school combo. Don't feel like a sandwich? Then at least try the chopped liver, which will be your go-to chopped liver recipe from now on. Still, let's not forget the unquestionable joy of fresh rye, kosher salami, pickles and a sandwich you can really sink your teeth into.

FOR THE CHOPPED LIVER:

2 large eggs

2 medium onions, thinly sliced

2 Tbsp olive oil

1 lb chicken livers, rinsed and patted dry

Kosher salt and pepper to taste

FOR THE SANDWICHES:

8 slices beef salami

8 slices double-rye bread

½ small red onion, thinly sliced into rounds

2 sour dill pickles, sliced lengthwise

¼ cup Russian-style mustard or honey mustard

1. To make the chopped liver, bring a medium pot of water to a boil, then lower heat to a simmer and carefully add the eggs to the pot. Cook, uncovered, for 12 minutes. Drain the pot and rinse the eggs under cool water. Peel the eggs and set aside.

2. In a large pan over medium-low heat, cook the onions in olive oil, stirring often, for 25-30 minutes, or until deeply caramelized. Add the cleaned chicken livers (any connective tissue should be removed) to the pan with the onions and cook for 6-7 minutes, or until browned and cooked through (a little pink is okay). Season well with salt and pepper. Let cool for 5 minutes, then add the eggs and contents of the pan to a food processor and pulse until combined but not pasty—two to three short pulses. Taste again for seasoning and transfer to a bowl. Cover well with plastic wrap touching the liver so that it doesn't discolor, and refrigerate until cool.

3. Heat a medium pan over medium-high heat. Add the salami and cook until seared, about 1 minute per side. Generously spread four slices of rye with chopped liver. Top each with two slices of salami, then some red onion rounds and pickle slices. Spread the top slice with mustard and cover the sandwiches. Enjoy at once.

Crispy Duck Salad

Duck used to be a big thing in Jewish households, but it went out of style around the turn of the last century. It's such a decadent meat that you may think it's not kosher, but it is. With crisp-skinned breasts served on a bed of fresh citrus, arugula and endive, all drizzled with a lovely dressing, it may become a new Friday-night favorite.

2–3 large boneless, skin-on duck breasts (3 lb total)

Kosher salt and pepper to taste, divided

1 large seedless navel orange

1 Tbsp honey

2 shallots, finely chopped

6 Tbsp red wine vinegar

2 Tbsp orange marmalade

½ cup olive oil

3 heads Belgian endive

6 cups baby arugula

½ cup slivered almonds, lightly toasted

2 Tbsp cilantro, roughly chopped

1. Preheat the oven to 350°F.

2. Score the skin and fat on the duck breasts in a crisscross motion without cutting into the actual flesh. Season with salt and pepper. Place the duck breasts, skin side down, in a large, cold ovenproof skillet, preferably a cast-iron pan. Turn the burner on to medium heat and cook the breasts for 6–8 minutes, or until the skin is crisp and golden and most of the fat is rendered off. Pour off the fat and place the skillet, with the duck breasts skin side up, in the preheated oven for another 6–10 minutes. The meat should be pink and tender in the center. Remove the duck from the pan and rest on the counter, tented with foil.

3. Zest the orange and set the zest aside. Peel the orange, then cut in half and thinly slice.

4. To make the dressing, heat the honey in a small saucepan over medium heat until it just starts to caramelize (watch it closely so that it doesn't burn). Remove from the heat, add the shallots, vinegar, marmalade and orange zest, and return to low heat. Stir to combine. Remove from the heat, whisk in the olive oil, season to taste and set aside.

(continued)

5. Slice the bottom ½ inch off of each Belgian endive and discard, leaving the remaining leaves whole.

6. Arrange the arugula, endive and sliced oranges on a large platter. Drizzle on some dressing. Slice the duck breasts and fan the pieces over the salad. Sprinkle with almonds and cilantro, and drizzle with more dressing before serving.

Caramelized Salmon Fillets

If you've had it up to here with salmon, try this Vietnamese take on Judaism's favorite fish. It's sweet and spicy, with a finishing crunch of fried shallots and herbaceous cilantro. Side it with rice to complete the feast.

4 (5–6 oz) boneless, skin-on salmon fillets

5 Tbsp loosely packed brown sugar

3 Tbsp water

2 tsp peanut or vegetable oil

2 Tbsp soy sauce

1 red chili, stemmed, seeded and finely chopped

2 cloves garlic, finely chopped

1 tsp pepper

2 Tbsp crispy fried shallots (store-bought at Asian markets or homemade)

2 Tbsp roughly torn cilantro leaves

1. Coat the flesh side of the salmon with the sugar and refrigerate for 30 minutes.

2. Add the water and oil to a large (not nonstick) skillet set over medium-high heat. As soon as it bubbles and sizzles, add the soy sauce, chili and garlic. Lower the heat to medium-low, season the sugar-coated salmon with pepper, then place the fish in the skillet, skin side down. Cook, uncovered, for about 3–4 minutes, then flip to the other side (scraping any stuck chili and garlic back into the sauce) and cook until the top of the salmon (the flesh side) is caramelized, about another 3–4 minutes, depending on the thickness of the fillets.

3. Remove the salmon from the skillet and place on a warm serving dish, skin side down. Spoon any remaining sauce from the pan overtop and sprinkle with crispy shallots and fresh cilantro.

Summer Squash Quiche

Pastry can be tricky, but don't let that stop you from making this show-stopping quiche. Just keep the dough chilled and you'll keep your cool. It's so worth it. The crisp shell is loaded with a vegetable-flecked filling with the tang of cheese and the taste of summer. It's like the heydays of the 1980s, in your mouth.

FOR THE PASTRY:

2 cups flour

¾ cup cold butter, cut into small pieces

½ tsp sea salt

2 Tbsp freshly grated Parmigiano-Reggiano

3–4 Tbsp ice-cold water

Vegetable oil spray

FOR THE FILLING:

2 tsp olive oil

1 small onion, diced

1 small summer squash (yellow zucchini), diced

1 cup sweet corn kernels (fresh is best, but frozen and thawed is fine)

Sea salt and pepper to taste

3 large eggs, beaten

1 cup whipping cream

1 cup shredded sharp white Cheddar

1. To make the pastry, place the flour in a large bowl, then add the butter and rub in with your fingertips until the mixture resembles fine breadcrumbs. Stir in the salt and Parmigiano-Reggiano, then slowly add the ice-cold water until the dough comes together. Knead briefly on a floured surface and form it into a flat disk. Wrap in plastic wrap and chill for 30 minutes.

2. Place the oil in a medium skillet set over medium heat, then sauté the onions in the oil for 2–3 minutes. Add the squash and sauté 5 minutes more. Stir in the corn and cook for 3 more minutes. Season with salt and pepper. Set aside to cool.

3. Remove the chilled pastry from the fridge. Lightly flour a work surface and roll out the dough until it's large enough to fill a 9-inch springform pan. Spray the pan with vegetable oil, then carefully place the dough into the pan, pressing until even on the

bottom and sides and up to the rim. Trim off the excess on top of the rim with a sharp knife. Refrigerate for 20 minutes.

4. Preheat the oven to 375°F. Prick the bottom of the tart shell all over with a fork. Place the springform pan on a baking sheet. Lightly press a large piece of foil into the pan, over the dough, and line evenly with 2 cups dry beans or rice for blind baking, making sure they're encased by foil. Bake the tart shell on the middle rack of the oven for 20 minutes. Remove the foil and beans. (Reserve the beans for your next blind-baking project.) Bake for 15 minutes more, or until very lightly browned.

5. Reduce the heat to 325°F. Set the tart shell aside.

6. In a medium bowl, whisk together the eggs, cream and a good pinch of salt, then stir in the cooled vegetable mixture. Sprinkle half of the cheese on the bottom of the crust, pour in the filling and top with the remaining cheese. Bake for 45–50 minutes, or until golden and just set. Let rest for at least 10 minutes before serving. This is also nice at room temperature along with a crisp green salad.

Rainbow Trout Tacos

SERVES

6

Next time you feel like eating fish, try these. Local trout is simply marinated before being pan-fried. Then it's tucked into tortillas and pumped up with an herbaceous mayo and zingy slaw for the best-ever Taco Tuesday.

FOR THE PICKLED SLAW:

½ head red cabbage, cored and very thinly sliced (about 4 cups)

½ red onion, very thinly sliced

2 cups apple cider vinegar

1 Tbsp sugar

¼ tsp sea salt

FOR THE MARINATED TROUT:

¼ cup olive oil

1 tsp dried oregano

1 tsp ground cumin

Sea salt to taste

1½ lb fresh boneless rainbow trout fillets (or salmon)

FOR THE CILANTRO MAYO:

1 cup mayonnaise

¼ cup milk

Juice of 2 limes (about ¼ cup)

¼ cup finely chopped cilantro

¼ tsp garlic powder

½ tsp sea salt

6 (4-inch) corn tortillas

Extra lime wedges, for garnish

1. For the slaw, combine the cabbage, onions, cider vinegar, sugar and sea salt in a nonreactive bowl. Stir well, cover and refrigerate for at least several hours before serving.

2. For the marinated trout, mix together the olive oil, oregano, cumin and salt. Pour over the fish and marinate in the fridge for 30 minutes.

3. Heat a large nonstick sauté pan over medium-high heat. Remove the trout from the marinade and place in the hot pan (no need to add extra oil). Season with salt.

4. Cook the fish for 4 minutes on the first side, then carefully flip the fillets and cook for another 2 minutes, or until cooked through. Remove the fish from the pan, peel away and discard the skin, and break the fish into large chunks.

5. For the cilantro mayo, combine the mayonnaise, milk, lime juice, cilantro, garlic powder and salt in a blender and blitz until smooth. Refrigerate until using.

6. Char the tortillas by toasting them in a dry pan until lightly charred on each side and pliable.

7. Divide the trout among the warm, charred tortillas. Top with the pickled slaw, drizzle with cilantro mayo and serve with a wedge of lime.

Pan-Seared Halibut with Romesco Sauce

Sear your favorite fish or grill up your favorite steaks or chicken, and char a bunch or two of green onions while you're at it. Then dip everything into this classic Catalan Romesco sauce. It's amazing what a simple sauce does to amp up a piece of fish, and there's no simpler side than charred green onions: brush them with olive oil, sprinkle with sea salt, throw on the barbecue until charred and enjoy.

FOR THE ROMESCO SAUCE:

8 small Campari tomatoes, slit with an X on top

3 cloves garlic, skin-on

Drizzle of olive oil plus ¼ cup, divided

3 Tbsp sliced almonds, toasted

¼ tsp red pepper flakes

¼ cup roasted sweet red peppers

1 slice toasted bread, torn into small pieces

1 Tbsp water

1 Tbsp sherry vinegar or red wine vinegar

Sea salt to taste

FOR THE FISH:

4 (8 oz) halibut fillets, about 2 inches thick (or other fresh firm whitefish)

Kosher salt and pepper to taste

2 Tbsp vegetable oil

Lemon wedges, for serving

1. Preheat the oven to 400°F.

2. To make the Romesco sauce, place the prepped tomatoes in a small baking dish along with the garlic cloves. Drizzle with olive oil and roast in the oven for 20 minutes. Remove from the oven and set aside to cool slightly. When cool enough to handle, remove the skins of the tomatoes and garlic, then transfer the veg to a food processor. Add the almonds, red pepper flakes, roasted red peppers, toasted bread, water and sherry vinegar. Blitz, slowly drizzling in the remaining ¼ cup olive oil, and puree until smooth. Add salt to taste. Cover the sauce and refrigerate until using.

3. Let the halibut stand at room temperature for 15 minutes before cooking. Line a plate with paper towel.

4. When ready to cook, pat the fish dry with paper towel and season generously with salt and pepper. In a large skillet over high heat, add the vegetable oil and heat until very hot. Carefully add the fillets and press down with a spatula to be sure there's good contact with the pan. Reduce the heat to medium and cook for 4–5 minutes, or until golden on one side, then flip and cook for 3–4 minutes more on the opposite side. Transfer to the paper towel–lined plate to drain off excess oil, and lightly season with salt. Serve with chilled Romesco sauce.

Bubi Fran's Meatloaf Surprise

My Bubi Fran was one of a kind. A businesswoman and a humanitarian, she owned lingerie stores, was a real estate agent and received the Order of Ontario, just to name a few of her many accomplishments. She was also an incredible bubi with a great smile and chuckle to match, and was the best cook in our large extended family—her food was full of schmaltz and love. This meatloaf was one of her signatures. It was years before I realized that most meatloaves don't have hard-boiled eggs running through their core.

2 lb lean ground beef (ground chicken or turkey also works well)

1 egg, beaten

1½ cups plain breadcrumbs

1 cup tomato sauce, divided

1 tsp Worcestershire sauce

½ cup warm water

Few shakes Tabasco sauce

1 pouch (about 1 oz) onion soup mix

3 slightly undercooked hard-boiled eggs (boiled for 8–10 minutes), peeled

1. Preheat the oven to 350°F. Spray a loaf pan with vegetable oil.

2. In a large bowl, combine the beef, egg, breadcrumbs, ¾ cup tomato sauce, Worcestershire, warm water, Tabasco and onion soup mix.

3. Place half of the mixture in the loaf pan and pat down. Then place the peeled eggs down the middle, end to end. Add the remaining meat mixture and pat down, making sure the eggs are completely covered. Top with the remaining ¼ cup tomato sauce.

4. Bake, uncovered, in the preheated oven for 1 hour. Let cool slightly before slicing and serving. Mashed potatoes and sweet peas are the perfect accompaniments.

Fried Liver & Onions

4

 We didn't grow up with fried foods in my parents' house. With a mom who's a dietitian and a dad who's a doctor, I literally had to go to Le Cordon Bleu to learn how to cook with fat. But there were a couple of occasions when my mom would pull out the avocado-green electric skillet. The first one was Chanukah, a joyous time, while the second one was the exact opposite. We'd come in from playing outside after school and smell hot oil. "Mmmm," we'd think. But then, with a spatula in her hand, my mom would appear in the door frame of the kitchen with a menacing smile on her face. "It's L.L. night," she'd say in a singsong voice. In case you were wondering, that stands for "liver lovers," which was obviously ironic. That said, if you were going to force kids to eat liver, I suppose this was the way to do it: coated and fried, then smothered with onions and mushrooms.

1 cup vegetable oil, divided

2 large sweet onions (such as Vidalia), halved and sliced

About 4 cups button mushrooms, halved

Sea salt and pepper to taste

4 thin slices (about 1½ lb) calves' liver

½ cup flour

2 eggs, lightly beaten

1½ cups panko breadcrumbs

¼ cup chopped flat-leaf parsley, for garnish (optional)

1. In a large skillet (or electric skillet), heat ½ cup oil over medium heat. Add the sliced onions and sauté until golden, stirring occasionally to avoid sticking, about 20–30 minutes. Add the mushrooms and sauté for 10–15 minutes longer. Season to taste with salt and pepper. Transfer the onions and mushrooms to a bowl, cover and set aside.

2. Rinse the liver in cold water and pat dry with paper towel. Season with salt.

3. Place the flour on a large plate, place the eggs on another plate and the panko crumbs on a third plate. Dredge each liver slice in flour, then dip in egg, then press into the panko. Set aside on a plate until ready to fry.

AMY ROSEN (178) KOSHER STYLE

4. In the same skillet used for the onions and mushrooms, heat the remaining ½ cup oil on medium. Once hot, add the liver and brown for 3–4 minutes per side, depending on the thickness of the slices and your preferred degree of doneness. While the liver cooks, line a clean plate with paper towel. When the liver is done, transfer it to the plate to drain on the paper towel.

5. Serve the liver smothered with mushrooms and onions and, if you like, sprinkled with parsley.

Classic Cabbage Rolls

What's red and green and sweet and sour? A classic dish from the old country (in this case, Poland) that has stood the test of time. Full of mildly spiced meat and rice and cooked in homemade tomato sauce until tender, cabbage rolls, for my money, rank among the top three of all cabbage-based comfort foods.

FOR THE ROLLS:

1 large head green cabbage

FOR THE SAUCE:

1 (28 oz) can crushed tomatoes

1 (15 oz) bottle chili sauce (such as Heinz)

¼ cup packed brown sugar

¼ cup honey

1 Tbsp Worcestershire sauce

3 Tbsp red wine vinegar

Juice of 1 lemon

FOR THE FILLING:

1 lb lean ground beef

½ cup raw long-grain white rice

½ tsp sea salt

¼ tsp pepper

½ tsp garlic powder

¼ tsp red pepper flakes

1 Tbsp Worcestershire sauce

1 egg, beaten

1. Preheat the oven to 350°F. Adjust the racks so that there's enough room for a large covered pot to fit in the center of the oven.

2. Core the cabbage and place the head in a large pot with a few inches of boiling water in the bottom. Cover and steam until the leaves separate easily, about 10 minutes. When cool enough to touch, carefully separate the leaves and drain on tea towels.

3. In a large ovenproof stockpot with a lid, make the sauce. Combine the crushed tomatoes, chili sauce, brown sugar, honey, Worcestershire, red wine vinegar and lemon juice. Stir well. Bring to a boil, then lower the heat and simmer, covered, for 20 minutes, stirring now and then.

(continued)

4. For the filling, combine the ground beef, rice, salt, pepper, garlic powder, red pepper flakes, Worcestershire and beaten egg. Mix well. (Your hands are the best tool for this.)

5. Now it's time to roll! Place a heaping tablespoon of filling in the center of each cabbage leaf, then tuck in the sides and roll it up, burrito style. Place each roll, seam side down, into the sauce. Keep tucking and rolling and placing into the sauce until all the beef mixture is gone. Cover the pot and cook in the preheated oven for 1 hour, or until the meat is tender and cooked through.

Honey-Garlic Chicken

A quick meal where all that's required are a few ingredients, some measuring and some dumping. It's chicken for people who don't like chicken. (But honestly, what's not to like about chicken?)

8 chicken thighs, patted dry

1 cup packed brown sugar

1 tsp dry mustard

4 cloves garlic, finely chopped

1 Tbsp finely chopped fresh ginger

3 Tbsp soy sauce

1 cup honey

1. Preheat the oven to 350°F.

2. Place the chicken pieces in a baking dish so that they fit snugly. Evenly sprinkle with the sugar, dry mustard, garlic, ginger and soy sauce, then top it all off with a glossy coat of honey.

3. Bake, uncovered, in the preheated oven for 40–50 minutes, or until the juices run clear. This dish is great with rice and edamame.

Friday-Night Roast Chicken

How to make the perfect roast chicken? I did the research, and this recipe takes its cues from Julia Child's famous bird, coupled with pointers from the food nerds at *America's Test Kitchen*. Roasting a chicken couldn't be easier, and is so much better than any supermarket rotisserie bird—especially since you can't transport that Friday-night aroma home.

1 (4–6 lb) roasting chicken	1 tsp kosher salt
2 Tbsp olive oil	Pepper to taste

1. Preheat the oven to 450°F.

2. Remove and discard anything you find in the chicken cavity and trim off excess skin and fat. Pat the chicken dry and rub with oil. Sprinkle with salt and pepper and massage it all in.

3. Place the chicken, breast side up, on a wire rack set over a roasting pan, tucking in the legs and wings. Roast, uncovered, in the preheated oven for 15 minutes. Carefully turn the chicken on its side and roast for another 10 minutes. The turning part is a bit of a balancing act; trussing the chicken with string adds stability. Either way is fine, though. Turn on the other side for another 10 minutes.

4. Reduce the heat to 350°F, turn the chicken breast side up again and roast for 30–40 minutes more. The general rule of thumb is about 1 hour of cooking for a 3-pound chicken, and an extra 10 minutes for each additional pound. A thermometer stuck into the meaty part of a leg (without touching the bone) should register at 165°F, the joints should feel loose and the juices should run clear. If this is all happening, remove the chicken from the pan and set aside on a cutting board, tented with foil, for 15 minutes.

5. Present your chicken on a large wooden cutting board, and let someone who knows what they're doing carve it up at the table. This could, in fact, be you.

Mu Shu Vegetables with Spring-Onion Pancakes

This is a variation on the classic Chinese dish with the handy wrappers and delightfully cloying hoisin sauce. There are two ways to do this: the easy way, and the not-as-easy way. For the latter, I'm providing you with the ingredients and know-how for making homemade Mandarin pancakes as mu shu wrappers, but these can also be found premade at most Asian groceries. Buying the wrappers is an excellent shortcut, although making them fresh is worth the effort. You've got to ask yourself, Do you have the time? The inclination?

FOR THE SPRING-ONION PANCAKES:

1½ cups plus 2 Tbsp flour, divided

¼ tsp sea salt

½ cup boiling water

3 Tbsp cold water

3 green onions, white part only, finely chopped

Sesame oil

FOR THE MU SHU VEGETABLES:

4 large eggs

1 tsp plus 1 Tbsp soy sauce, divided

¼ tsp pepper

1 tsp sugar

1 tsp grated fresh ginger

3 Tbsp vegetable oil, divided

1 red pepper, sliced into thin strips

2 carrots, julienned into matchstick-size strips

1½ cups shredded green cabbage

1 (8 oz) can sliced water chestnuts, drained

10 button mushrooms, halved

2 Tbsp sake

Jarred hoisin sauce, for serving

1. For the spring-onion pancakes, mix together 1½ cups flour and the salt in a medium bowl. Slowly pour the boiling water into the flour, stirring until it starts to come together. Add the cold water. Stir in the green onions and knead in the remaining 2 tablespoons flour. Knead the dough on your work surface until elastic, about 10 minutes, then shape into a ball. Put back into the bowl, cover with a damp tea towel and let sit for 20 minutes.

2. Meanwhile, start the mu shu vegetables. In a medium bowl, whisk together the eggs, 1 teaspoon soy sauce, pepper, sugar and ginger.

3. Heat a wok or large skillet over medium-high heat, then add 1 tablespoon oil, swirling the wok or skillet to coat, and heat until hot but not smoking. Stir-fry the beaten egg mixture until just cooked through, about 20 seconds. Transfer the eggs to a bowl and chop into bite-size pieces.

4. Do a quick wipe of the wok or skillet with some paper towel, then heat it up again, add another tablespoon of oil and swirl like before. When hot, add the prepared red peppers, carrots and cabbage and stir-fry for 1 minute. Add the water chestnuts and mushrooms and stir-fry for another minute. Transfer the vegetables to the bowl of cooked eggs.

5. Add the remaining tablespoon of oil to the wok and heat until hot. Add the egg and vegetable mixture along with the remaining 1 tablespoon soy sauce and the sake, and stir-fry until it's all hot and combined. Taste for seasoning.

6. Lightly flour your work surface and roll the pancake dough into a skinny 1-foot-long roll, about 1 inch in circumference. Cut the roll into 12 equal pieces, flatten each piece with your palm, then roll each piece into a 6-inch round with a rolling pin. Brush the entire surface of the pancake with sesame oil, on one side only, then stack two pancakes together, oiled side to oiled side (you'll see why in a minute).

7. Heat a large nonstick skillet over medium heat, and cook a couple of pancake stacks at a time for about 30 seconds on each side, or until a few brown spots appear and they bubble slightly. Remove the pancakes from the pan and separate the paired pancakes. (You cook them in pairs because they're so delicate that they would fall apart otherwise.) Repeat until all six stacks are cooked and you have 12 gorgeous wrappers. Cover with plastic wrap to keep them moist and warm.

8. To serve, put out the bowl of mu shu, lay the warm onion pancakes on a plate and pour some hoisin sauce into a bowl. Spread the hoisin on a pancake, fill with vegetable mu shu, fold and eat.

Maple-Soy Brisket

When feeding a crowd, especially around the holidays, this is my go-to main course. I've swapped out my usual "secret ingredient," Coca-Cola, for maple syrup, and the salt for soy, making for a Judeo-Canadian-Chinese take and a new classic in the making. Roast some veggies in a separate pan while you're at it.

1 cup pure maple syrup

½ cup soy sauce

½ cup apricot preserves

1 pouch (about 1 oz) onion soup mix

½ cup tomato sauce

Pepper to taste

1 (5 lb) beef brisket

1. In a small bowl, mix together the syrup, soy sauce, apricot preserves, onion soup mix, tomato sauce and pepper. Place the brisket in a roasting pan and pour the marinade overtop. Cover with foil and refrigerate overnight. If you don't have that much time to spare, several hours will do in a pinch.

2. When ready to cook, preheat the oven to 325°F. Cook the brisket, still covered with foil, for 3 hours. Remove the foil and cook, uncovered, for an additional 30 minutes. Let cool, then refrigerate the brisket (still in the pan); this aids in slicing.

3. When the brisket is cold, skim and discard the fat with a spoon. Remove the brisket from the sauce and slice thinly against the grain. Add it back into the pan with the sauce.

4. About 1 hour before you're ready to serve, preheat the oven to 350°F. Place the brisket in the oven and reheat, uncovered, for 20-30 minutes, spooning the sauce overtop a few times. Serve at once.

Chapter 5

A LITTLE SOMETHING
SWEET

(Pareve & Dairy)

Is This the Best Restaurant in America?

The setting is a circa-1975 basement on Chrystie Street in Manhattan's Lower East Side—past the Tenement Museum, beyond the Judaica shops and a couple of blocks over from Katz's Deli. Sammy's Roumanian Steak House exists here, where there's history on the outside, and even more of it on the inside.

I'm here with Shragit and her family. I met Shrag at Jewish summer camp when we were 16 years old. Her family is like my family. There's her dad, Sam, her mom, Fira, her husband, Steve, her younger brother, Mo, and his lovely wife, Rachel. I'm in town visiting, and tonight we're all out celebrating Sam and Fira's 49th anniversary. Mo, who has been at Sammy's before and happens to be the cantor at Congregation Emanu-El of New York, promises we're all in for an experience "that is a gastronomic and cultural journey into eastern European life." Born in Kaunas, Lithuania, when it wasn't a great place to be a Jew, Shragit and her family endured years of struggle before she and her parents escaped persecution and moved to Israel in 1972. Then it was on to South Africa, then Canada and finally New York City. Now they're part of this table of doctors, cantors and professional musicians, all living the American dream.

Dinner begins as soon as we sit down, when baskets of pickles hit the table: half sours, full sours and giant, juicy pickled tomatoes. Then comes the rye bread and the chopped liver, tossed tableside by a twenty-something T-shirted server, the liver mixed with radishes, crispy bits of chicken skin, deeply caramelized onions and a river of schmaltz (chicken fat). "Listen to the Jewish *shtetl* music," says Sam, closing his eyes and swaying to the muscle memory of playing similar strains on his own concert violin.

There's more golden schmaltz on the table in maple syrup–like pitchers, and the vodka we order is smacked down encased in ice, making the bottle entirely too easy to drink. The walls at Sammy's Roumanian are plastered with yellowing, curled pictures of famous New Yorkers like Matthew Broderick, and even more of drunken diners just like you and me. "It's like a party in your Russian bubbe's basement," says Mo.

The person responsible for the party is Dani Lubnitzki, known as Dani Luv. For the past 20 years, Luv has entertained guests with his musical stylings, lyrics and Casio keyboard. He sits and stands in a corner on a slightly raised platform with a dollar-store disco ball spinning overhead. Luv looks like the living embodiment of Krusty the Clown, and he has the Catskillian sense of humor to match. His rotating repertoire includes twists on standards such as "Strangers with My Wife," and a version of "Piano Man" that starts "It's nine o'clock on a Shabbos night." Meanwhile, "Hey Jude" is turned into "Hey Jew" easily enough, as Luv sings, "Take a sad song and make it sadder . . ."

After the chopped liver, the first of several restaurant-wide horas break out. Heads go through ceiling tiles as adults drunk on Stolichnaya hoist other adults up on chairs. (All of the duct tape suddenly makes sense.) "Start spreading the Jews, these Ashkenazis are wanting to stay . . ."

I can't tell you much about the main courses, because I'm too busy filling up on dills and chopped liver and am extra busy drinking and dancing and especially laughing. To be honest, I can't recall how my steak tastes, or if I even eat it. I do remember the sweet-and-sour cabbage rolls, because they taste like my Boobie Ronnie's, and that the fried silver-dollar potatoes are the perfect drunk food. Almost all the dishes we order hit like a wave of nostalgia usually reserved for weddings and funerals. It occurs to me that they're not after Michelin stars here. They're after hearts.

During the frenzied final round of "Hava Nagila," practically the whole restaurant is up and dancing, high on artery-clogging life. "What a surprise," chimes in Luv. "The *shiksas* are dancing and the Jews are eating." I'm not sure what's more delicious: the food or the shtick. "Amy, Amy," Sam yells to me, over the music, "you'll never find this anywhere else in the world. Only in America!" he beams.

And to think, all we had to do to get here was make a reservation.

Classic Rice Pudding

I've got to give a nod to *Fine Cooking* magazine for this one. When researching rice pudding, I fell down an Internet rabbit hole and came out the other side with my take on its recipe—I couldn't believe how much it tasted like my favorite commercial brand of rice pudding. Not too fatty, easy to make and as soothing as all get-out, it's the rice pudding of yesteryear.

4 cups whole milk

½ cup medium-grain white rice

2 large egg yolks

⅓ cup sugar

2 tsp vanilla extract

¼ tsp ground cinnamon, plus more for garnish

1. Heat a large, heavy saucepan over high heat, then add the milk and rice. Bring to a boil, stirring constantly, then lower heat and simmer, covered and stirring now and then, for 15 minutes. Uncover and continue simmering, stirring frequently, for 10 minutes more, or until the rice is tender.

2. In a small bowl, whisk together the egg yolks, sugar, vanilla and cinnamon. Slowly whisk into the rice pudding mixture and heat on medium-low, stirring until the mixture has thickened, about 2 minutes. Remove from the heat and transfer to a serving bowl. Cover with plastic wrap touching the top of the pudding so a skin doesn't form. Refrigerate for at least 30 minutes. Before serving, dust with a touch more cinnamon.

Chocolate Malted Meringues

If you love chocolate, malt and texture, these meringues will hit all of your sweet spots in equal measure. Easy to make and impressive to look at, they're a special treat that one can imagine a nostalgic French woman enjoying.

3 egg whites, room temperature

¾ cup plus 2 Tbsp sugar

Pinch of sea salt

1 tsp vanilla extract

2 Tbsp icing sugar

2 Tbsp malted powder (such as Horlicks)

1 Tbsp cocoa powder

1. Preheat the oven to 300°F and line a baking sheet with parchment paper.

2. Place the egg whites in a large clean bowl. Using an electric beater or stand mixer, whisk until soft peaks form, about 2–3 minutes. While continuously beating, add 1 tablespoon of sugar at a time, leaving about 10 seconds between each addition. Once all the sugar is incorporated and the meringue mixture is firm and glossy, whisk in the salt, vanilla and icing sugar.

3. In a small bowl, mix the malted powder and cocoa together until combined, then sprinkle over the meringue mixture and gently fold in.

4. Form six large mounds of meringue using 2 heaping tablespoons of mixture for each one and spacing them well apart on the prepared baking sheet. Bake for 20 minutes. Turn off the oven but do not remove the meringues or even open the door. Let the meringues cool completely in the oven for at least 1 hour before serving.

Lemon Meringue Pie with Coconut Crust

SERVES

8

I started out by making this with a straight-up graham cracker crust, which you're more than welcome to do. But then I thought, what if we upped the tropical side of this zesty pie? Graham crackers meet coconut meet lemon meet meringue—meet my mouth.

FOR THE CRUST:

1½ cups graham cracker crumbs

1½ cups sweetened shredded coconut

6 Tbsp butter, melted

FOR THE FILLING AND MERINGUE:

1 (10 oz) can sweetened condensed milk

3 eggs, separated

¾ cup fresh lemon juice

5 Tbsp sugar

1. Preheat the oven to 350°F and grease a 9-inch tart pan.

2. For the crust, in a medium bowl, combine the graham crumbs, coconut and butter. Stir to combine, then press the mixture into the greased tart pan, pressing it evenly on the bottom and up the sides. Bake for 10–12 minutes, or until lightly golden. Set aside.

3. For the filling, in a medium bowl, whisk together the sweetened condensed milk, egg yolks and lemon juice. Beat for several minutes until smooth and glossy. It will be runny.

4. Pour the filling into the crust, place the tart pan on a baking sheet and bake for 25–30 minutes, or until just set. Remove the tart from the oven and let cool for 30 minutes.

5. In a medium bowl, whisk the egg whites until foamy, then slowly add in the sugar. Continue whisking until stiff peaks form, then spoon onto the baked, cooled pie. Turn on the broiler setting for the oven, then broil for about 30 seconds, or until the meringue slightly browns—watch it very closely to prevent burning. Let the tart cool for 1 hour before slicing and serving.

Kichel: Rainbow Nothings

I always thought these airy cookies were fried, because they were so crisp and light—hence the name "nothings." I made these with my wee nieces, and looking into the little ladies' bright three-year-old and six-year-old eyes, I thought, what could make these sugary *kichel* even better? Colorful sprinkles, of course.

3 Tbsp sugar

1 tsp sea salt

4 eggs

9 egg yolks

¾ cup vegetable oil

2 tsp vanilla extract

3½ cups flour, plus extra for kneading

FOR THE COATING:

3 cups sugar

½ cup colored sprinkles

1. In a stand mixer fitted with the paddle attachment, combine the sugar, salt, eggs, egg yolks, vegetable oil, vanilla and flour. Beat on low speed for 15–20 minutes, until the dough is smooth and the gluten is developed. Note: This will be the stickiest dough you've ever felt.

2. Preheat the oven to 350°F and line two baking sheets with parchment paper.

3. Generously flour your work surface and tip the dough onto the flour. Knead by hand for 3–5 minutes, or until the dough is no longer sticky. Scatter a bit more flour on the work surface and place the dough on top, then cover with plastic wrap and let sit for 30 minutes. Wipe away any excess flour so that the work surface is ready for the next step.

4. Combine the sugar and sprinkles in a bowl. Spread half the mixture on your work surface and roll the dough out to ¼-inch thickness. Sprinkle the rest of the sugar-sprinkle mixture on top of the dough. Press and flip until nicely coated. Using a sharp knife, slice the dough into 1 × 2-inch rectangles, pressing the dough into more of the sugar. Then twist each rectangle into a bowtie and place them 1 inch apart on the prepared baking sheets.

(continued)

5. Bake for 25–30 minutes, or until golden brown. Remove the cookies to wire racks and let cool and dry thoroughly for 4 hours. Store in airtight containers for up to 1 week.

Note: With the leftover egg whites and the leftover sprinkle sugar, make rainbow meringues (page 197)! Just omit the malted powder and cocoa.

Apricot-Almond Rugelach

MAKES

4

DOZEN

These are all about the tender cream-cheese dough, and the scant apricot and almond filling. My mom's friend, Etty, who had a kosher baking business, is who I got my love of rugelach from, while French patisseries gave me an appreciation for these flavors; so I combined the two. These perfect little crescent shapes go down well with a warm cup of tea and some company.

2 cups flour

1 cup cold butter, chopped

1 block (8 oz) full-fat cold cream cheese, chopped

3 Tbsp sugar

2 tsp vanilla extract

FOR THE FILLING:

½ cup smooth apricot jam

½ cup blanched slivered almonds, toasted

FOR THE TOPPING:

2 Tbsp cane or demerara sugar

½ tsp ground cinnamon

1 egg, beaten, for egg wash

1. For the dough, place the flour, butter, cream cheese, sugar and vanilla in a food processor. Pulse until a uniform large ball forms. Divide into three equal balls and wrap each in plastic wrap. Refrigerate for at least 3 hours or, even better, overnight.

2. To prepare the filling, warm the jam in a small pot over low heat or in the microwave for 30 seconds. Set aside. In a bowl, crush the toasted almonds with your hands, or place them in a resealable plastic bag and crush with a rolling pin.

3. To prepare the topping, mix the sugar with cinnamon in a small bowl and set aside.

4. Line two baking sheets with parchment paper. Remove the dough from the fridge about 30 minutes before using. On a well-floured surface, roll out one of the dough balls into a large circle, about 12 inches in circumference and about ⅛ inch thick. Repeat with the remaining two dough balls.

5. Preheat the oven to 350°F.

(continued)

6. Using a knife or pizza cutter, slice each circle into 16 wedges and separate them slightly. Evenly divide the jam and almonds among the three circles (this comes out to about ½ teaspoon jam and a pinch of nuts per rugelach), leaving ½ inch clean at the outer edges. Roll the wedges into crescents by rolling the wider outer edge in toward the point.

7. Place on the baking sheets, at least 1 inch apart, with the point sides down. Brush the tops of the rugelach with beaten egg and sprinkle with the cinnamon sugar.

8. Bake in the middle of the oven for 20–22 minutes, or until golden brown. These can be stored in an airtight container at room temperature for up to 1 week.

Classic NYC Egg Cream

SERVES

1

When you research traditional Jewish dishes, you realize New York bears the torch for many of the cultural classics, including some recipes that didn't quite make it to Canada. The egg cream is one such treat; it contains neither egg nor cream, but tastes like a fizzy melted Fudgsicle.

3 Tbsp chocolate syrup (recipe follows; or store-bought)

¼ cup milk

About ¾ cup soda water

1. Pour the chocolate syrup and milk into a tall glass. While beating vigorously with a spoon, stream in the cold soda water until the glass is almost full. Serve at once and sip away.

Chocolate Syrup

MAKES 2 CUPS

½ cup cocoa powder

1 cup milk

2 cups sugar

Pinch of sea salt

½ tsp vanilla extract

1. In a medium saucepan over medium-low heat, whisk together the cocoa powder and milk. Add the sugar and whisk until the sugar is completely dissolved. Bring to a boil, while constantly stirring, for 3 minutes. Remove from the heat and add the salt and vanilla. Stir to combine. Let cool completely, then pour into a clean jar and refrigerate.

Toblerone-Chunk *Hamantaschen*

It's not Purim until you've had these famous triangular cookies, shaped and named after the hat worn by Haman (the bad guy in the book of Esther, a tyrannical leader who faced off against Esther, who then rose up against him and became a voice of the people). My cookie take is based on looking over at a Toblerone bar while developing recipes and having a eureka moment: Toblerone chunks are already triangular! I'm not saying I'm another Esther or anything, but let's rise up together and make these chocolatey *hamantaschen*!

1½ cups butter, room temperature

½ cup sugar

1 egg

½ tsp vanilla extract

1 Tbsp milk

3¼ cups flour

1 tsp baking powder

½ tsp kosher salt

2 (3½ oz) Toblerone bars, broken into triangles

1. In a food processor, pulse the butter with the sugar until smooth. Add the egg, vanilla and milk and blend to puree.

2. In a medium bowl, whisk together the flour, baking powder and salt. Add to the processor and pulse until the dough comes together. It will be sticky. Scoop the dough onto plastic wrap and cover well, shaping into a flat disk. Refrigerate for at least 3 hours, but it's best left overnight.

3. Remove the dough from the fridge 1 hour before using.

4. Preheat the oven to 375°F and line two baking sheets with parchment paper.

5. On a well-floured surface, roll the dough out to ⅛ inch thick. The dough is very tender, so work quickly and add more flour to the work surface if it starts sticking. Cut into 3-inch circles (fluted is extra nice).

(continued)

6. Place one triangle of Toblerone on its side in the center of each circle, then, using your fingers, wet the edges of the circle and pull them up to form a triangle around the piece of Toblerone, pinching the corner edges so they hold together, but leaving an opening in the center. Place the prepared *hamantaschen* on the baking sheets and bake for 12–15 minutes, or until lightly golden.

Chocolate Babkas

Some people like cinnamon babka, but I'm a chocolate person. Like I always say, "If it ain't chocolate, it ain't dessert." This babka skirts the line between bread and cake, snack and dessert, and though it's not the moistest loaf around, its beauty shines even brighter when griddled with butter the next day.

FOR THE DOUGH:

3 Tbsp warm water

3 Tbsp sugar, divided

1 Tbsp active dry yeast

⅔ cup milk, warmed

2 eggs

¼ cup melted butter, cooled

3½ cups flour

½ tsp sea salt

FOR THE FILLING:

½ cup butter, room temperature

½ cup semisweet chocolate chips

¼ cup sugar

Pinch of sea salt

FOR THE TOPPING:

¼ cup flour

2 Tbsp sugar

4 tsp cold butter

1 egg, for egg wash

1. In the bowl of a stand mixer fitted with a dough hook, combine the warm water, 1 teaspoon sugar and the yeast. Let stand for 10 minutes, until foamy. Add the milk, two eggs and melted butter. Stir to combine. Add the flour, remaining sugar and salt, and mix at low speed for 3–4 minutes. Scrape down the sides of the bowl and continue mixing at medium speed for 6–7 minutes, until the dough is glossy, elastic and not sticky.

2. Transfer the dough to a large well-oiled bowl and cover with a tea towel. Let sit for 1 hour in a warm, draft-free area, until doubled in size.

3. Line two baking sheets with parchment paper. Set aside.

(continued)

4. For the filling, place the butter, chocolate chips, sugar and salt in a bowl and mix until combined. Set aside.

5. For the topping, place the flour, sugar and butter in a small bowl and use your fingertips to mix until crumbly. Set aside.

6. On a lightly floured surface, roll out the dough into a large rectangle about 15 × 11 inches. Spread the filling evenly over the dough, leaving a clean border all around. Roll the dough lengthwise into a tight log, then cut the log in half down the middle. You now have two stumpy logs.

7. Working with one log at a time, cut in half lengthwise and lay each half side by side, cut side up. Pinch the top ends together, then twist the two halves together, like a spiral. Pinch the bottom ends together. Repeat with the second log.

8. Transfer the babkas to the prepared baking sheets. Cover with tea towels and let rise for 30 minutes, or until noticeably puffed up.

9. Preheat the oven to 375°F.

10. Whisk the remaining egg and brush overtop of the babkas. Sprinkle with the streusel topping.

11. Bake in the preheated oven for 30–35 minutes, or until golden brown. Let cool for at least 30 minutes, then slice and enjoy. This is also great when griddled with butter after a couple of days. Or, dip in beaten eggs and milk: Hello babka French toast!

Wildflower-Honey Cake

SERVES
10–12

A sweet New Year on Rosh Hashanah means dipping apples in honey and eating honey cake. This one is full of floral wild honey and sprinkled with flowers, making for not just a sweet but also a beautiful treat. The good thing about honey cake is that it stays unusually fresh on the counter for several days. Maybe it's because of all the good wishes and intentions.

3½ cups flour

¼ tsp sea salt

1½ tsp baking powder

1 tsp baking soda

1 tsp ground cinnamon

¼ tsp nutmeg

4 eggs

¾ cup sugar

½ cup vegetable oil

1¾ cups wildflower honey, plus extra for drizzling

½ cup strong coffee, cooled

1 cup blanched sliced almonds, toasted

Edible flowers, for garnish (optional)

1. Remove the top oven rack so that the cake will have room to rise. Preheat the oven to 325°F and spray a Bundt pan with cooking spray.

2. In a large bowl, combine the flour, salt, baking powder, baking soda, cinnamon and nutmeg. Set aside.

3. Using a stand mixer fitted with the paddle attachment, beat the eggs, then add the sugar. Continue beating until thicker and lighter in color, about 2–3 minutes. Add the oil, honey and coffee, blend well, then slowly add in the dry ingredients. Beat until smooth, then stir in the almonds.

4. Pour into the greased Bundt pan and bake for 1 hour, or until a cake tester inserted in the center comes out clean. Cool the cake in the pan for 20 minutes, then invert onto a wire rack to cool completely. Drizzle with 1–2 tablespoons honey and sprinkle with edible flowers (if using), which will stick to the honey. Slice and serve for a happy New Year.

Poppy Seed (*Mohn*) & Sesame Cookies

MAKES

3

DOZEN

Buttery and tender with the snap of a shortbread and the flavor of your favorite Jewish bakery, these are traditional *mohn* cookies. Poppy seeds are an Ashkenazi mainstay, finding their way into breads but mostly into desserts like *hamantaschen*, babkas and strudels. I was thinking of bagels, and also tahini, when it occurred to me to combine the two here, so I decided to add some sesame seeds to the mix.

1½ cups flour

¼ tsp sea salt

1 cup icing sugar

2 Tbsp poppy seeds

1 Tbsp sesame seeds

2 Tbsp water

1 tsp vanilla extract

¾ cup butter, room temperature.

1. Place the flour, salt, icing sugar, poppy seeds and sesame seeds in a bowl and stir to combine. Add the water, vanilla and butter, and work it together with your clean hands until a uniform dough comes together.

2. Transfer the dough to plastic wrap and form a 12-inch log. Refrigerate until firm, at least 3 hours.

3. Preheat the oven to 350°F and line two baking sheets with parchment paper.

4. Unwrap the dough and slice into ¼-inch disks. Place the cookie slices on the baking sheets 1 inch apart. Bake for 6 minutes, then rotate the trays 180 degrees and bake for another 6–8 minutes, or until the edges just start to brown. Let cool on the baking sheets, then munch away.

Coconut-Lime Macaroons

MAKES

12

A citrus twist gives these sweet macaroons a pie-like vibe, while the finishing touch of salt makes them as addictive as cookies, which they basically are. This is the classic treat that my friends and I used to sneak into movie theaters when we were keeping kosher for Passover.

1 egg white

2 Tbsp lime zest

½ cup sweetened condensed milk

2½ cups sweetened shredded coconut

Pinch of sea salt

1. Preheat the oven to 325°F and line a baking sheet with parchment paper.

2. In a bowl, whisk together the egg white, lime zest and sweetened condensed milk. Stir in the coconut until thoroughly combined.

3. Spoon 12 heaping tablespoons of coconut mixture onto the baking sheet, 1 inch apart. Sprinkle with salt. Bake the macaroons until golden, about 20 minutes. Let cool completely on the baking sheets before serving.

Winter Compote

Great for a Seder dessert (or as part of a breakfast to get things moving) and fab for Tu B'Shevat or any old Shabbat, compote is a good way of reminding everyone how delicious chocolate is. Just kidding. This is compote for people who hate compote.

1 cup dried pitted prunes

1 cup dried apricots

1 cup dried cranberries

¼ cup packed brown sugar

2 strips lemon rind

½ tsp ground cinnamon

¼ tsp ground cardamom

½ cup toasted chopped walnuts (optional)

1. Place the prunes, apricots and cranberries in a medium saucepan with enough water to cover. Bring to a boil, then reduce to a simmer and cook, covered, for about 15 minutes, stirring now and then.

2. Add the brown sugar, lemon rind, cinnamon and cardamom. Cook, uncovered, for 10 minutes, stirring often, until the fruit is soft and the syrup is thick. Remove from the heat and discard the lemon rind. Chill the compote for several hours. Sprinkle with walnuts if desired. This is nice with brie and crackers too.

Blueberry Crumble Pie

MAKES

1

(9-INCH)
PIE

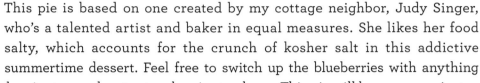

This pie is based on one created by my cottage neighbor, Judy Singer, who's a talented artist and baker in equal measures. She likes her food salty, which accounts for the crunch of kosher salt in this addictive summertime dessert. Feel free to switch up the blueberries with anything from raspberries to peaches to strawberries to plums. This pie will become a mainstay in your repertoire, as it has in mine.

FOR THE CRUST:

2 cups flour

½ tsp kosher salt

2 Tbsp sugar

¾ cup canola oil

1 Tbsp vanilla extract

2 Tbsp milk

FOR THE FILLING:

5 cups fresh blueberries

Juice of ½ lemon

¼ cup sugar

1 Tbsp flour

1 Tbsp cornstarch

FOR THE CRUMBLE TOPPING:

½ cup flour

3 Tbsp packed brown sugar

2 Tbsp sugar

½ tsp kosher salt

2 Tbsp cold butter

1 tsp vanilla extract

1. Preheat the oven to 350°F.

2. To make the crust, place the flour, salt and sugar in a 9-inch pie plate. Stir in the oil, vanilla and milk. Work together into a patty of dough (the dough will be quite moist), and remove ¼ cup, setting it aside for the crumble topping.

3. Press the remaining dough evenly into the pie plate, making sure it isn't too thick on the bottom. Prick the bottom of the crust all over with a fork, then place the pie plate on a baking sheet and bake until very lightly golden, about 12 minutes. Remove and set aside.

4. To make the filling, combine the blueberries with the lemon juice, sugar, flour and cornstarch. Mix thoroughly and pour into the prepared piecrust. It will be quite full.

5. Raise the oven temperature to 425°F.

6. Put the crumble topping ingredients (the flour, both sugars and salt) into a bowl. Using your fingers, blend in the butter until the mixture is crumbly. Add the vanilla and the ¼ cup reserved piecrust dough, blending it in with your fingers. Mound the crumble topping overtop of the blueberries.

7. Bake on a baking sheet for 15 minutes, then lower the heat to 375°F for another 25–30 minutes, or until the pie is golden. Let cool for several hours before eating.

Carrot-Zucchini Bread with Vanilla Cream-Cheese Frosting

1

LOAF

It's not health food, but it's good food. Loaded with vegetables and the crunch of pecans, it also oozes sweetness and has a decadent cream-cheese frosting. Seriously, make this loaf.

2 cups flour

2 tsp ground cinnamon

½ tsp baking soda

¼ tsp baking powder

¼ tsp sea salt

1 cup sugar

1 cup packed brown sugar

¾ cup vegetable oil

3 eggs

1 tsp vanilla extract

1 cup grated zucchini (about 1 medium)

1 cup grated carrot (about 1 medium)

1 cup pecan pieces, toasted and cooled

FOR THE FROSTING:

¼ cup butter, softened

½ block (4 oz) full-fat cream cheese, softened

1 tsp vanilla extract

1½ cups icing sugar

1. Preheat the oven to 350°F. Butter and flour a 9 × 5 × 3-inch loaf pan.

2. Place the flour, cinnamon, baking soda, baking powder and salt in a medium bowl and whisk together. In a separate large bowl, beat both sugars, the oil, eggs and vanilla until noticeably lighter and well combined. Stir in the zucchini and carrots. Add the flour mixture and pecans, and stir well.

3. Transfer the batter to the prepared loaf pan, and set the loaf pan on a baking sheet. Bake until the top is golden brown and a cake tester inserted in the center comes out clean, about 1 hour and 20 minutes. Remove from the oven and set the pan on a wire rack to cool for 15 minutes. Then run a knife around the loaf to loosen it, turn it out onto the rack and let it cool completely.

4. For the frosting, in a medium bowl, beat the softened butter and cream cheese with a hand mixer until smooth and fluffy, about 2-3 minutes. Stir in the vanilla, then the icing sugar. Cover and chill until using.

5. To serve, spread and swirl the chilled cream-cheese frosting overtop of the bread. Slice and enjoy.

AMY ROSEN (224) KOSHER STYLE

Chocolate-Caramel-Almond Matzo Brittle

10–12

Passover commemorates the exodus of the Israelites from ancient Egypt. So you've got Moses, the parting of the Red Sea, the Ten Commandments and a triumphant return to Canaan (I'm sure you've seen the movie). Passover also means lots of unleavened recipes, some of which are little miracles in and of themselves, including this sweet treat. From Bonnie Stern to Joan Nathan, everyone has a secret recipe for this winning chocolate-caramel snack, and who's to say who invented it? (Although Bonnie Stern credits Marcy Goldman, a Montreal baker.) A *bisl* of this, a *shmeck* of that, and before too long it's time for chocolate brittle, a treat so good it's almost worth wandering the desert for.

6 sheets egg matzo

½ cup sliced almonds (optional)

1 cup butter

1 cup packed brown sugar

2 cups semisweet chocolate chips (or your favorite high-quality chocolate, chopped)

Pinch of finishing salt (such as Maldon)

1. Preheat the oven to 350°F and line a large baking sheet with foil. Arrange the matzo in a single layer on the foil, but don't worry if they overlap slightly.

2. If using almonds, toast them in the medium saucepan you're about to use for the butter and sugar mixture (one less pot to clean). Once toasted, remove the almonds from the pan and set aside.

3. Place the butter and brown sugar in the saucepan and bring to a boil. Go against your instincts and try not to stir it. Just cook for a few minutes until the mixture comes together and looks saucy, then pour it evenly over the matzo. Bake the matzo in the oven for about 10 minutes, or until the caramel is bubbling.

4. As soon as the matzo comes out of the oven, sprinkle with the chocolate chips. Wait 5 minutes, then spread the chocolate as evenly as possible with a spatula, making sure to get under the overlapped pieces. Sprinkle toasted almonds (if using) and salt overtop, then pop in the fridge until the chocolate and caramel are set, about 15 minutes. Break into chunks and serve.

Foolproof Flourless Chocolate Cake

The primary symbol of Passover is the matzo, a mouth-parching unleavened bread that stands in for the breadstuffs that the Israelites ate during their flight from slavery. Now, I'm not saying this decadent chocolate cake is the equivalent to the parting of the Red Sea or anything, but it is a mini miracle during this most unleavened of holidays.

1 lb good-quality bittersweet chocolate

1½ cups butter, room temperature

2 tsp vanilla extract

1 cup sugar

1 cup ground almonds

2 Tbsp Amaretto liqueur (optional)

6 eggs, separated

Pinch of sea salt

Berries, for garnish (optional)

1. Preheat the oven to 300°F and grease a 9-inch springform pan. Wrap the bottom and sides of the pan in foil to catch any batter.

2. Chop up the chocolate and melt in the microwave on medium heat in 20-second intervals, stirring in between and being careful that it doesn't burn. If you don't have a microwave, slowly melt the chocolate in a pan on the stove over low heat, stirring often. When the chocolate has melted, stir in the butter, vanilla, sugar, almonds and Amaretto (if using). Set aside to cool.

3. In a bowl, beat the egg yolks until they are thick and bright yellow, about 2-3 minutes. Stir them into the cooling chocolate mixture.

4. In a separate clean bowl, beat the egg whites with a pinch of salt until stiff peaks form, about 3-4 minutes, then fold them into the chocolate mixture a little at a time until you've got a nice even chocolatey batter. Don't overmix the batter.

5. Pour the batter into the prepared springform pan and bake in the preheated oven for 1 hour. The middle will rise and crack a bit, but that's normal. Remove from the oven and let the cake rest for 1 hour before removing it from the pan. It's a very moist cake, so slicing it with a sharp wet knife is advisable. Garnish with berries, if using.

The author's parents, Marsha and Fred, get hitched.

Cherry-Hazelnut *Mandelbroit*

Also known as Jewish biscotti, *mandelbroit* is a crunchy cookie made for dipping in coffee or tea. Stud it with fruits and nuts, roll it in cinnamon sugar, dip it in chocolate—you can take the flavors anywhere you want them to go. Just keep the additions finely chopped to make for easy slicing later on.

¾ cup dried cherries

3 eggs

1 cup vegetable oil

1½ cups sugar

1 tsp vanilla extract

3 cups flour

½ cup large-flake oats

1 cup chopped toasted, skinned hazelnuts

1 tsp baking powder

1 tsp sea salt

1. Preheat the oven to 350°F and line two baking sheets with parchment paper.

2. Soak the cherries in hot water for 20 minutes. Drain, pat dry with a paper towel and finely chop.

3. In a stand mixer, combine the eggs, oil, sugar and vanilla. Beat to combine. Add the flour, oats, hazelnuts, baking powder and salt. Beat again until just combined. Stir in the cherries.

4. Divide the dough into three logs approximately 12 inches long × 2½ inches wide. Place them on the prepared baking sheets and bake for 25–30 minutes. They should be firm but will still be pale. Remove from the oven and cool for 5 minutes.

5. Lower the oven temperature to 300°F.

6. Using a sharp knife, slice on the diagonal into ¾-inch pieces and place back on the baking sheets, cut side up, 1 inch apart.

7. Bake for 30–35 minutes, or until golden brown. Store at room temperature in a sealed container for up to 1 week.

Ten Menus

There are a lot of recipes in this book. There are a lot of Jewish holidays and *simchas* in a calendar year. Let's put them all together and create menus that are just right for you. Here are some suggestions.

Vegetarian Shabbat:

Roasted Butternut Squash Soup, p. 66
Hummus with Zhug, p. 89
Quinoa-Tofu Bowl with Greens & Green Goddess, p. 140
Carrot-Zucchini Bread with Vanilla Cream-Cheese Frosting, p. 224

Seder with a Twist:

Roasted Salmon with Horseradish Sauce & Pickled Onions, p. 137
Honey-Harissa Roasted Carrots, p. 81
Bibb Lettuce with Root Chips, p. 113
Honey-Garlic Chicken, p. 183
Sweet & Sour Meatballs, p. 145
Winter Compote, p. 220

Dairy Break-Fast:

Bialys: Soft Onion Buns, p. 21
Vegetarian "Chopped Liver," p. 43
Creamed Herring, p. 40
Spinach Bites with Honey Mustard, p. 117
Pickled Salmon, p. 17
Amy's Perfect Pecan Buns, p. 51

Swellegant High Holidays:

Mom's Sweet Challah, p. 19
Crisp Cucumber & Radish Salad, p. 120
Kasha Pilaf, p. 109
Pan-Seared Halibut with Romesco Sauce, p. 174
Maple-Soy Brisket, p. 188
Wildflower-Honey Cake, p. 215

It's Chanukah:

Warm Marinated Olives, p. 123
The Big Salad, p. 101
Miami Ribs, p. 146
Lacey Latkes & Applesauce, p. 99
Cherry-Hazelnut *Mandelbroit*, p. 231

Sunday Brunch:

Joanna's Famous Granola, p. 25
Veggie Cream Cheese, p. 31
Honey-Mustard Gravlax, p. 47
Israeli Salad & Homemade Labneh, p. 110
Sour Cream-Pecan Coffee Cake Muffins, p. 35

Classic Sabbath:

Instant Pickles, p. 125
Matzo Balls, p. 64
Chicken Soup (aka Jewish Penicillin), p. 69
Orange & Carrot Salad, p. 105
Crispy Smashed Baby Potatoes with Malt Vinegar, p. 85
Friday-Night Roast Chicken, p. 185
Kichel: Rainbow Nothings, p. 201

A Nosh for a Bris:

Double-Decker Egg & Tuna Party Sandwiches, p. 48
Summer Squash Quiche, p. 170
The Best Caesar Salad, p. 97
Greek Orzo Salad, p. 106
PB&J Bread Pudding, p. 44

Dishes to Bring for Mourners:

Cheese Blintzes with Blueberry Sauce, p. 39
Split Pea & Noodle Soup, p. 65
Sour Cream & Onion Potato Knishes, p. 82
Skillet Kugel, p. 90
Apricot-Almond Rugelach, p. 203

Sukkot Cornucopia:

Cabbage Borscht, p. 59
Dukkah-Dusted Carrot Fritters with Herbed Yogurt, p. 114
Pickled Beet Salad, p. 118
Four-Ingredient Weeknight Chicken, p. 150

Four kids and a fireplace: the early years.

Acknowledgments

You probably realize that books don't just appear out of thin air. It takes a lot of people with a lot of talent to bring a book as nice as this one to life. So for starters, I'd like to thank one of the most wonderful people I've ever met, my editor Zoe Maslow, for immediately understanding my cookbook concept, embracing it with relish (or maybe *chrain* is more appropriate) and pushing it through with an enthusiasm only matched by my equally gifted publisher, Robert McCullough.

Do you like the photography in this book? It's pretty amazing, right? I'm here to tell you that this book would not be what it is without the brilliance, speed and humor of photographer Ryan Szulc, and prop stylist Madeleine Johari. This is the third cookbook I've done with them and I can't imagine working with anyone else.

The freshly made food was shopped for, prepared and styled by Michelle Rabin, who was my intern when I was Food Editor at *Chatelaine*, but she's now better than me at everything. Michelle's assistant, Vanessa Robak, was also a massive help in the kitchen. For five days in May 2018, with *schnozes* to the grindstone, we cooked, we baked, we shot photos, we laughed, and boy, did we ever eat.

You know how they say never meet your heroes? Well I met mine and she illustrated the essays in this book. I could not believe my good fortune when Alanna Cavanagh said yes to collaborating on this cookbook, and then I couldn't believe my eyes when I saw the perfect illustrations she drew and inked.

Thanks to Kristin Cochrane for embracing this *Yiddishe* idea on behalf of Penguin Random House Canada, the supremely creative *shiksa* Terri Nimmo for the book design, Susan Burns for being such a keen managing editor, Brittany Larkin for being such a great production manager and, of course, you wouldn't even know about this book were it not for the efforts of the top-notch sales, marketing and publicity teams, and my agent Hilary McMahon.

Who else? Well, without my parents, I don't exist, so neither does this book. Thank Fred and Marsha Rosen next time you see them! I'd also like to thank my mom and Judy Singer for basically writing the "On Eating Kosher" rules, because they were terrified I would screw it up. Also, big-ups to the rest of the Rosen clan, including my brothers and their partners and my sweet nieces and nephews, plus friends, near and dear, here and there, for their encouragement, *fressing* and feedback.

Finally, I'd like to thank the following people, places and things, who inspired some of these recipes, including (in no particular order) Marsha Rosen, Marlene Axmith, Irit Salem, Joanna Sugar, Judy Singer, Anita and Cyril Press, Andrea Sugar, Paulina Glazman, Rayna Morris-Cullin, Diet Coke, Bubi Fran, Boobie Ronnie, Dana Levitt, Harbord Bakery, United Bakers Dairy Restaurant, Noreen Gilletz, *Seinfeld*, Lucy Waverman, Israel, Bonnie Stern, Canada, America, Poland, Russia and, as always, chocolate.

Index